Verbs

&

Essentials
of Grammar

Second Edition

Simone Oudot

Mc
Graw
Hill

New York   Chicago   San Francisco   Lisbon   London   Madrid   Mexico City
Milan   New Delhi   San Juan   Seoul   Singapore   Sydney   Toronto

5   6   7   8   9   0   DSH/DSH   0   1   0

ISBN 978-0-07-184136-8

McGraw-Hill books are available at special quantity discounts to use as premiums and sales promotions, or for use in corporate training programs. For more information, please write to the Director of Special Sales, Professional Publishing, McGraw-Hill, Two Penn Plaza, New York, NY 10121-2298. Or contact your local bookstore.

This book is printed on acid-free paper.

Preface

French Verbs and Essentials of Grammar is a practical handbook and guide to the principal grammatical concepts of the French language for learners at any level of proficiency. Concepts are presented in a logical order and concise manner so that students with no more than one semester of French can follow the explanations. More advanced students—even those who have gained considerable mastery—will find this an excellent quick reference, study and review guide, or grammatical brush-up aid. This book can be used as a basis for group work, individual study, or simply as a classroom or personal reference.

Part I focuses on the mastery of French verbs. The chapter on pronunciation at the beginning of the section gives a good introduction for beginners to the sounds of the language. In subsequent chapters, all tenses and conjugations of verbs are presented, with extensive, easy-to-use verb charts and clear explanations. Correct use of tense and mood as well as sequence of tenses are also covered in this section. In this way, learners master correct usage, as well as simply learn to conjugate verbs.

Part II presents concise explanations of other essential points of French grammar, including articles, pronouns, interrogatives and exclamations, prepositions, and much more. The examples chosen to illustrate each concept were selected for authenticity. They are phrases and sentences frequently used in contemporary, idiomatic French, providing clear illustrations of current usage.

For classwork or for personal reference, *French Verbs and Essentials of Grammar* is a versatile and easy-to-use guide to French grammar. It is a useful tool for learners seeking not only to learn verb tenses and grammar points but also to master correct usage. For learners at any level, *French Verbs and Essentials of Grammar* can help pave the way to mastery of the French language.

Part One:
French Verbs

Contents

1. Pronunciation

There are 37 sounds in French corresponding to 37 symbols of the International Phonetic Alphabet.

Vowels

[i] il, vie, Sylvie
[a] patte, carte
[ɑ] pâte, basse
[ɛ] tête, bête, laide, merci
[e] blé, quai
[ɔ] sotte, robe

[o] dôme, sot, beau, gauche
[u] cou, roue
[y] mur, vendu, eu
[ə] le, fenêtre, je
[œ] œuf, jeune, peur
[ø] feu, creux, œufs

Nasals

[ã] an, Jean, lent
[ɛ̃] pin, pain, plein

[ɔ̃] bon, rond, ombre
[œ̃] un, brun, lundi

Consonants

[p] pas, prix, soupe
[t] tôt, très, vite
[k] cas, qui, kilo, sac
[f] feu, photo, neuf
[s] sel, dessous, sceau, nation, ceux
[ʃ] chaud, chemin, tâche
[b] bateau, beurre, rabais
[d] dent, direction, aide
[g] Gabriel, gâteau, bague

[v] vin, rêve,
[z] rose, désert, zéro
[ʒ] neige, jaune
[l] là, lune, sol
[r] rat, rire, venir
[m] mal, méchant, dame
[n] nez, nid, sonner
[ɲ] montagne, chataigne
[ŋ] camping, parking

Semi-Consonants

[j] yeux, soleil, pied
[w] oui, moi, ouate

[ɥ] huile, cuire

The Alphabet

a	[a]	h	[aʃ]	o	[o]	v	[ve]
b	[be]	i	[i]	p	[pe]	w	[dublə-ve]
c	[se]	j	[ʒi]	q	[ky]	x	[iks]
d	[de]	k	[ka]	r	[er]	y	[i-grɛk]
e	[ə]	l	[el]	s	[es]	z	[zɛd]
f	[ef]	m	[em]	t	[te]		
g	[ge]	n	[en]	u	[y]		

Accents

´	l'accent aigu	é gives the sound	[e]
`	l'accent grave	è gives the sound	[e]
^	l'accent circonflexe	ê gives the sound	[e]
••	le tréma Noël	[noel]	

1. *Le tréma* means that the preceding vowel must be pronounced separately.

2. The *accent grave* over *a* and *u* does not affect the sound of the vowels: *à* [a]; *où* [u].

3. The *accent circonflexe* over *a* affects the sound of this vowel slightly, sometimes not, depending on the speaker's dialect.

château = [ʃato]   or [ʃɑto]

Rhythm and Intonation

1. In French, syllables are not stressed as they are in English. Instead, there tends to be a slight stress on the last syllable of a sentence or phrase. As a result, each syllable has equal length, except the last one, but the pause is very slight.

Nous allons déjeuner.
Nous allons déjeuner chez Suzanne.
Après les courses, nous allons déjeuner chez Suzanne.
Après les courses, mon mari et moi, nous allons déjeuner chez Suzanne.

2. In general, the intonation in French is dictated by the speaker's feelings. However, a general rule is that there is a falling intonation at the end of an affirmative or a negative sentence. In interrogative sentences, there is falling intonation at the end of a question asking for information and rising intonation at the end of a yes/no question.

Où vas-tu?   Veux-tu du lait?

Qu'est-ce que tu fais?   Irez-vous dans les Alpes cette année?

Comment va votre mère?   Est-ce que tu as réussi à ton examen?

Punctuation Marks

,	la virgule		!	le point d'exclamation
.	le point		( )	la parenthèse
:	les deux points		« »	les guillemets
;	le point virgule		'	l'apostrophe
. . .	les points de suspension		-	le trait d'union
?	le point d'interrogation		—	le tiret

Punctuation in French is much the same as in English, with some differences.

1. *Les guillemets* « » replace English quotation marks.

Comme La Fontaine l'a dit:« Rien ne sert de courir, il faut partir à point ».	As La Fontaine said: "It's no use to run, if you did not start on time."

2. A dash (*tiret*) is used to set off the words spoken by different speakers in a dialogue.

— Il fait beau, dit Paul. On sort?	"The weather is good," said Paul. "Shall we go out?"

2. Regular Verbs — The Simple Tense Forms

The Infinitive

Regular French verbs are classed according to the endings of the infinitive: the first conjugation (verbs whose infinitives end in -er); the second conjugation (-ir verbs); and the third conjugation (-re verbs). -Er verbs constitute a majority of French verbs.

parler to speak   **finir** to finish   **vendre** to sell

When the ending of the infinitive is dropped, what is left is called the stem. The sets of endings that are added to the stem or to the infinitive to denote person, number, tense, and mood are called conjugations.

Simple Tenses of the Indicative Mood

1. Present   Le présent
2. Imperfect   L'imparfait
3. Simple Past   Le passé simple
4. Future   Le futur

Conditional Mood

5. Present Conditional   Le présent du conditionnel

Imperative Mood

6. Imperative   Le présent de l'impératif

Subject Pronouns

For a detailed discussion of subject pronouns, see Chapter 20. Remember that the subject of the verb is of first, second, or third person, singular or plural.

	Singular		Plural	
1st person	je (j')	I	nous	we
2nd person	tu	you	vous (formal singular)	you
			vous (plural)	you
3rd person	il	he	ils (m.)	they
	elle	she	elles (f.)	they
	on	one, we, they, people		

The Present

First Conjugation, -*er* Verbs

The present tense expresses an action or a state that is taking place at the moment of speech. There is a difference in the notion of time between English and French. While French expresses time at the precise moment the action is taking place, English most often acknowledges the duration of the action. *Je parle français* is the equivalent of both "I am speaking French" and "I speak French." English also uses an emphatic expression, *I do speak,* which does not exist in French.

The present tense in French is formed by adding the appropriate endings to the stem of the infinitive.

parler, to speak

je parl*e*	I speak, am speaking	**nous** parl*ons*	we speak, are speaking
tu parl*es*	you speak, are speaking	**vous** parl*ez*	you speak, are speaking
il parl*e*	he speaks, is speaking	**ils** parl*ent*	they speak, are speaking
elle parl*e*	she speaks, is speaking	**elles** parl*ent*	they speak, are speaking
on parl*e*	we, they, people speak, are speaking; one speaks		

A noun, pronoun, or a combination of a noun and a pronoun may be used as the subject of the verb form.

Je parle **français.**	I speak French. I do speak French.
Anne et moi, nous parlons **anglais.**	Anne and I speak English.
Elles parlent **à Paul.**	They are speaking to Paul.
Les enfants parlent **mal.**	The children speak badly.
On parle **des vacances.**	We are talking about vacation.

Negative Form

To form the negative, place *ne* (*n'*) before the verb and *pas* after the verb. (See Chapter 24.)

Je *ne* **parle** *pas* **espagnol.**	I don't speak Spanish.
Tu *ne* **parles** *pas* **bien.**	You are not speaking well.
On *ne* **parle** *pas* **de toi.**	We are not talking about you.

Sample Verbs of the First Conjugation

aider to help	**monter** to go up, to climb
aimer to love, to like	**montrer** to show
apporter to bring	**oublier** to forget
arriver to arrive	**parler** to speak, to talk
chanter to sing	**passer** to pass
commencer to begin, to start	**penser** to think
demander to ask	**porter** to carry, to wear
donner to give	**préparer** to prepare
entrer to enter, to go in	**raconter** to tell
étudier to study	**regarder** to look at
fermer to close	**rester** to stay
habiter to live	**tourner** to turn
inviter to invite	**travailler** to work
jouer to play	**trouver** to find

Second Conjugation, -*Ir* Verbs

finir, to finish
I finish, am finishing, etc.

Singular	Plural
je fin*is*	**nous fin***issons*
tu fin*is*	**vous fin***issez*
il	**ils**
elle } **fin***it*	**elles** } **fin***issent*
on	

Je *finis* **mes devoirs.**	I am finishing my homework.
Jean *finit* **son repas.**	Jean is finishing his meal.
Où *finissez*-**vous vos vacances?**	Where are you ending your vacation?
Nous *finissons* **nos achats.**	We are finishing our shopping.
Elles *finissent* **leur voyage à Rome.**	They are finishing their trip in Rome.

Sample Verbs of the Second Conjugation

atterrir to land	**languir** to languish
brunir to brown, to tan	**maigrir** to grow thin
démolir to demolish, to pull down	**obéir** to obey
élargir to widen	**pourrir** to rot
finir to finish	**raccourcir** to shorten
fleurir to bloom	**ralentir** to slow down
gémir to groan, to moan	**réfléchir** to think over
grandir to grow tall	**remplir** to fill, to fill out
grossir to grow bigger	**réunir** to gather
guérir to recover	**réussir** to succeed
investir to invest	**rôtir** to roast

Third Conjugation, -re Verbs

vendre, to sell
I sell, am selling, etc.

Singular	Plural
je vend*s*	nous vend*ons*
tu vend*s*	vous vend*ez*
il (elle, on) vend	ils (elles) vend*ent*

Je *vends* ma maison.	I am selling my house.
Vendez-vous du beurre?	Do you sell butter?
Nous *vendons* aussi des œufs.	We also sell eggs.
Elles *vendent* des écharpes.	They sell scarves.
Ils ne *vendent* rien.	They sell nothing.

Sample Verbs of the Third Conjugation

attendre	to wait for	**pondre**	to lay (eggs)
défendre	to defend, to forbid	**répandre**	to spread, to spill
descendre	to go down	**répondre**	to answer
entendre	to hear	**rendre**	to give back
épandre	to spread	**tendre**	to stretch
fondre	to melt	**tondre**	to shear, to mow (grass)
mordre	to bite	**vendre**	to sell
pendre	to hang		

Sample Present Tense Sentences

Je *travaille* dans un bureau.	I work in an office.
Alice *vend* sa voiture.	Alice is selling her car.
Nous ne *regardons* pas la télévision.	We are not watching television.
Comment *trouvez*-vous Jacques?	How do you like Jacques?
Ils *montent* au premier.	They are going up to the second floor.
Les Dupont n'*habitent* pas à Nice.	The Duponts do not live in Nice.
Josette *obéit* à ses parents.	Josette obeys her parents.
Vous *jouez* au bridge?	Do you play bridge?
Tu *portes* une jolie robe.	You are wearing a pretty dress.
Elles nous *invitent* à rester.	They invite us to stay.

The Imperfect

There are two simple past tenses in French, the imperfect (*imparfait*) and the simple past (*passé simple*). Their uses vary.

The imperfect is the tense of description. It describes an action or a state that took place in the past, without defining its duration or its time of completion.

Il *habitait* Londres pendant la guerre.	He lived in London during the war.

But when one indicates the duration, another past tense must be used (*passé composé* or *passé simple*).

Il *a habité* (*il habita*) **Londres pendant dix ans.**	He lived in London for ten years.

The imperfect is also used to express a habitual action or an action that occurred repeatedly in the past.

Elle *tondait* **la pelouse tous les jours.**	She mowed the lawn every day.

The imperfect is used to describe physical or mental states that existed in the past.

Il *avait* **mal à la tête et ne se** *souvenait* **de rien.**	He had a headache and remembered nothing.

The imperfect tense is formed by adding the appropriate endings to the first person plural of the indicative tense (minus the *-ons*).

parler (*parlons*)
I was speaking, used to speak, etc.

je parl*ais*	nous parl*ions*
tu parl*ais*	vous parl*iez*
il (elle, on) parl*ait*	ils (elles) parl*aient*

finir (*finissons*)
I was finishing, used to finish, etc.

je finiss*ais*	nous finiss*ions*
tu finiss*ais*	vous finiss*iez*
il (elle, on) finiss*ait*	ils (elles) finiss*aient*

vendre (*vendons*)
I was selling, used to sell, etc.

je vend*ais*	nous vend*ions*
tu vend*ais*	vous vend*iez*
il (elle, on) vend*ait*	ils (elles) vend*aient*

Je *demandais* **son adresse.**	I was asking his address.
Il *travaillait* **dur.**	He was working hard.
Nous *parlions* de vous.	We were talking about you.
Alice et Jacqueline *obéissaient* **toujours.**	Alice and Jacqueline obeyed always.
Vous *défendiez* les pauvres.	You used to defend poor people.
C'est le bruit que nous *entendions*.	That's the noise we used to hear.

See Chapter 10, Sequence of Tenses (page 47), for an explanation of the uses of the *imparfait* versus the *passé composé*.

The Passé Simple

The *passé simple* (simple past tense) expresses an action or a state that occurred at a specific time in the past. It is used only in writing and is usually found in literature. Its equivalent in conversation is the *passé composé*, a perfect tense. (See Chapter 3.)

The simple past tense is formed by adding the appropriate endings to the stem of the infinitive.

<table>
<tr><td colspan="2" align="center">**parler**
I spoke, did speak, etc.</td><td colspan="2" align="center">**finir**
I finished, did finish, etc.</td></tr>
<tr><td>je parl*ai*</td><td>nous parl*âmes*</td><td>je fin*is*</td><td>nous fin*îmes*</td></tr>
<tr><td>tu parl*as*</td><td>vous parl*âtes*</td><td>tu fin*is*</td><td>vous fin*îtes*</td></tr>
<tr><td>il (elle, on) parl*a*</td><td>ils (elles) parl*èrent*</td><td>il (elle, on) fin*it*</td><td>ils (elles) fin*irent*</td></tr>
</table>

<table>
<tr><td colspan="2" align="center">**vendre**
I sold, did sell, etc.</td></tr>
<tr><td>je vend*is*</td><td>nous vend*îmes*</td></tr>
<tr><td>tu vend*is*</td><td>vous vend*îtes*</td></tr>
<tr><td>il (elle, on) vend*it*</td><td>ils (elles) vend*irent*</td></tr>
</table>

Je me *préparai* à partir.	I prepared myself to leave.
Il *entra* sans frapper.	He came in without knocking.
Nous *perdîmes* notre chemin.	We lost our way.
Les lilas *fleurirent* tôt.	The lilacs bloomed early.
Les voitures *passèrent* à toute vitesse.	The cars passed by at high speed.

The Future

The future tense is formed by adding the future endings to the infinitive of *-er* and *-ir* verbs. For *-re* verbs, the *e* is dropped before adding the endings.

<table>
<tr><td colspan="2" align="center">**parler**
I will speak, etc.</td><td colspan="2" align="center">**finir**
I will finish, etc.</td></tr>
<tr><td>je parler*ai*</td><td>nous parler*ons*</td><td>je finir*ai*</td><td>nous finir*ons*</td></tr>
<tr><td>tu parler*as*</td><td>vous parler*ez*</td><td>tu finir*as*</td><td>vous finir*ez*</td></tr>
<tr><td>il (elle, on) parler*a*</td><td>ils (elles) parler*ont*</td><td>il (elle, on) finir*a*</td><td>ils (elles) finir*ont*</td></tr>
</table>

<table>
<tr><td colspan="2" align="center">**vendre**
I will sell, etc.</td></tr>
<tr><td>je vendr*ai*</td><td>nous vendr*ons*</td></tr>
<tr><td>tu vendr*as*</td><td>vous vendr*ez*</td></tr>
<tr><td>il (elle, on) vendr*a*</td><td>ils (elles) vendr*ont*</td></tr>
</table>

J'*apporterai* les sandwichs.	I'll bring the sandwiches.
Tu *étudieras* tout l'été.	You'll study all summer.
Les fruits *pourriront*.	The fruits will rot.
Nous *réfléchirons* à votre proposition.	We'll think about your proposal.
Vous *défendrez* votre pays.	You'll defend your country.

The Conditional Mood

The endings of the present conditional are, like those of the future tense, added to the whole infinitive.

parler		**finir**	
I would speak, etc.		I would finish, etc.	
je parler*ais*	nous parler*ions*	je finir*ais*	nous finir*ions*
tu parler*ais*	vous parler*iez*	tu finir*ais*	vous finir*iez*
il (elle, on) parler*ait*	ils (elles) parler*aient*	il (elle, on) finir*ait*	ils (elles) finir*aient*

vendre	
I would sell, etc.	
je vendr*ais*	nous vendr*ions*
tu vendr*ais*	vous vendr*iez*
il (elle, on) vendr*ait*	ils (elles) vendr*aient*

1. The conditional usually expresses an eventuality. The cause or condition for this eventuality can be implicit or explicit.

The eventuality can be contained in a *si*-clause, in which case it is explicit.

Si tu parlais plus fort,	If you spoke louder,
on t'entendrait.	we would hear you.
Je grossirais si je mangeais plus.	I would put on weight if I ate more.
Si vous m'invitiez, je resterais.	If you invited me, I would stay.

When the eventuality is implied in the conditional clause, the cause and condition are implicit.

Aimeriez-vous être balayeur de rues?	Would you like to be a street sweeper?
Auriez-vous l'audace de m'accuser de	Would you be so audacious as to
voler?	accuse me of stealing?

2. The conditional is also used to make a request or a refusal more polite.

J'aimerais te parler.	I would like to speak to you.
Je ne voudrais pas la voir.	I would not want to see her.

3. The conditional also expresses probability or conjecture.

Il vendrait sa maison.	He is probably selling his house.
Est-ce qu'elle l'achèterait?	Would she buy it?

The Imperative Mood

The imperative takes its forms from the second person singular of the indicative present (verbs in -*er* drop the -s) and from the first and second person plural of the indicative present. The imperative is a mood of action. It is used to command or persuade, with the intent of prompting a result.

parler	finir	vendre
parle	finis	vends
parlons	finissons	vendons
parlez	finissez	vendez

Parle à ton voisin!	Speak to your neighbor!
Finissons notre travail!	Let's finish our work!
Vendez votre voiture à Charles!	Sell your car to Charles!

Endings of Simple Tenses

Indicative Mood

	-er		-ir		-re	
Present	*stem* e	____ ons	____ is	____ issons	____ s	____ ons
	____ es	____ ez	____ is	____ issez	____ s	____ ez
	____ e	____ ent	____ it	____ issent	____	____ ent
Imperfect	____ ais	____ ions	____ ais	____ ions	____ ais	____ ions
	____ ais	____ iez	____ ais	____ iez	____ ais	____ iez
	____ ait	____ aient	____ ait	____ aient	____ ait	____ aient
Passé Simple	____ ai	____ âmes	____ is	____ îmes	____ is	____ îmes
	____ as	____ âtes	____ is	____ îtes	____ is	____ îtes
	____ a	____ èrent	____ it	____ irent	____ it	____ irent
Future	*infinitive* ai	____ ons				
	____ as	____ ez				
	____ a	____ ont				

Conditional Mood

Present	*infinitive* ais	____ ions
	____ ais	____ iez
	____ ait	____ aient

Imperative Mood

Present	____ e	____ is	____ s
	____ ons	____ issons	____ ons
	____ ez	____ issez	____ ez

Verb Synopsis

In a synopsis any one form of the verb is given in all the tenses.

parler - je

Indicative	Simple Tenses	Translation
Present	je parle	I speak, I am speaking
Imperfect	je parlais	I used to speak, was speaking
Passé Simple	je parlai	I spoke
Future	je parlerai	I will speak
Conditional Present	je parlerais	I would speak
Imperative (*tu* form)	parle!	speak!

3. Regular Verbs — Auxiliary Verbs and the Perfect Tenses

The perfect (compound) tenses are formed with a simple tense form of one of the auxiliary verbs (*avoir* or *être*) and a past participle.

The perfect tenses are:

1. Present Perfect	Le passé composé
2. Pluperfect	Le plus-que-parfait
3. Preterite Perfect	Le passé antérieur
4. Future Perfect	Le futur antérieur
5. Past Conditional	Le conditionnel passé

Simple Tenses of *Avoir* and *Être*

avoir	Present	Imperfect	Passé Simple
to have	j'ai	j'avais	j'eus
	tu as	tu avais	tu eus
	il (elle, on) a	il (elle, on) avait	il (elle, on) eut
	nous avons	nous avions	nous eûmes
	vous avez	vous aviez	vous eûtes
	ils (elles) ont	ils (elles) avaient	ils (elles) eurent

	Future	Conditional
	j'aurai	j'aurais
	tu auras	tu aurais
	il (elle, on) aura	il (elle, on) aurait
	nous aurons	nous aurions
	vous aurez	vous auriez
	ils (elles) auront	ils (elles) auraient

être	Present	Imperfect	Passé Simple
to be	je suis	j'étais	je fus
	tu es	tu étais	tu fus
	il (elle, on) est	il (elle, on) était	il (elle, on) fut
	nous sommes	nous étions	nous fûmes
	vous êtes	vous étiez	vous fûtes
	ils (elles) sont	ils (elles) étaient	ils (elles) furent

	Future	Conditional
	je serai	je serais
	tu seras	tu serais
	il (elle, on) sera	il (elle, on) serait
	nous serons	nous serions
	vous serez	vous seriez
	ils (elles) seront	ils (elles) seraient

The auxiliary verb *avoir* is used with the majority of verbs.

J'ai **mangé une pomme.**	I ate an apple.
Nous *avons* **maigri cette année.**	We lost weight this year.

However, the following verbs take the auxiliary *être*. Nearly all these verbs describe motion.

Infinitive	Past participle
aller to go	**allé**
arriver to arrive, to happen	**arrivé**
descendre to go down, to come down	**descendu**
devenir to become	**devenu**
entrer to enter, to go in	**entré**
monter to climb, to go up	**monté**
mourir to die	**mort**
naître to be born	**né**
partir to leave	**parti**
rentrer to go back, to go home	**rentré**
rester to stay, to remain	**resté**
retourner to return	**retourné**
revenir to come back	**revenu**
sortir to go out	**sorti**
tomber to fall	**tombé**
venir to come	**venu**

Elle *est tombée* **dans l'escalier.**	She fell in the stairs.
Il *est né* **le premier décembre.**	He was born on December 1st.

The verbs *descendre, monter, rentrer,* and *sortir,* when used as transitive verbs (which take a direct object), are conjugated with *avoir*.

Nous *avons descendu* **les valises.**	We took the suitcases downstairs.

The Past Participle

A past participle is formed by adding -*é* to the stem of an -*er* verb, -*i* to the stem of an -*ir* verb, and -*u* to the stem of an -*re* verb.

parler	**parl**é	spoken, talked
finir	**fin**i	finished
vendre	**vend**u	sold

NOTE: See Chapter 8, Irregular Verbs, for irregular past participles.

The Passé Composé

The *passé composé* is formed with the present tense of *avoir* or *être* and a past participle. It is used to describe an action or a state that happened in the past at a precise moment. See Chapter 10, Sequence of Tenses, for an explanation of the *imparfait* versus the *passé composé*.

parler I spoke, I talked, etc.

j'ai parlé   nous avons parlé
tu as parlé   vous avez parlé
il (elle, on) a parlé   ils (elles) ont parlé

sortir I went out, etc.

je suis sorti(e)   nous sommes sorti(e)s
tu es sorti(e)   vous êtes sorti(e)(s)
il (elle, on) est sorti(e) ils (elles) sont sorti(e)s

Il m'a donné un cadeau.   He gave me a present.
Vous êtes allés en Italie.   You went to Italy.

NOTE: In compound tenses, the negative is placed on either side of the auxiliary verb.

Nous *n'*avons *pas* vendu la voiture.   We did not sell the car.

Agreement with the Past Participle

Verbs Using *Avoir* as the Auxiliary

If a verb is conjugated with *avoir,* the past participle agrees with the direct object, *if* the direct object precedes the verb. The direct object can be a personal pronoun, the relative pronoun *que* at the beginning of a relative clause, or the interrogative or exclamative pronouns *quel* or *lequel.*

Où sont mes lunettes? Tu *les* as   Where are my glasses? You put them
   pos*ées* sur la table.   on the table.
Thérèse? Oui, c'est *elle* que j'ai   Thérèse? Yes, it is she that I
   invit*ée.*   invited.
Quels *fruits* as-tu mang*és*?   What fruits did you eat?

Verbs Using *Être* as the Auxiliary

If the verb is conjugated with *être,* the past participle agrees with the subject of the verb.

Elle est partie à cinq heures.   She left at five.
Nous étions arrivés à l'heure.   We had gotten there on time.
Marc sera allé chez moi.   Marc will have gone to my home.

The Pluperfect

The *plus-que-parfait* is formed with the imperfect of *avoir* or *être* and a past participle.

parler I had spoken, etc.

j'avais parlé	nous avions parlé
tu avais parlé	vous aviez parlé
il (elle, on) avait parlé	ils (elles) avaient parlé

venir I had come, etc.

j'étais venu(e)	nous étions venu(e)s
tu étais venu(e)	vous étiez venu(e)(s)
il (elle) était venu(e)	ils (elles) étaient venu(e)s

Jean a dit qu'il t'avait donné son livre.	Jean said that he had given you his book.
Les Martin avaient déjà dîné.	The Martins had already eaten.
Elle était entrée sans frapper.	She had gone in without knocking.

The Preterite Perfect

This tense is formed with the *passé simple* of *être* or *avoir* and a past participle. Like the *passé simple*, this tense is used only in literary works.

finir I finished, etc.

j'eus fini	nous eûmes fini
tu eus fini	vous eûtes fini
il (elle, on) eut fini	ils (elles) eurent fini

aller I went, etc.

je fus allé(e)	nous fûmes allé(e)s
tu fus allé(e)	vous fûtes allé(e)(s)
il (elle, on) fut allé(e)	ils (elles) furent allé(e)s

Quand j'eus fini de parler, ils entrèrent.	When I had stopped speaking, they came in.
Nous fûmes arrivés avant tous les autres.	We arrived before everybody else.

The Future Perfect

The future perfect is formed with the future of *être* or *avoir* and a past participle.

vendre I will have sold, etc.

j'aurai vendu	nous aurons vendu
tu auras vendu	vous aurez vendu
il (elle, on) aura vendu	ils (elles) auront vendu

arriver I will have arrived, etc.

je serai arrivé(e)	nous serons arrivé(e)s
tu seras arrivé(e)	vous serez arrivé(e)(s)
il (elle, on) sera arrivé(e)	ils (elles) seront arrivé(e)s

J'aurai fini mes valises à huit heures.	I will have finished my suitcases at eight o'clock.
Nous serons partis avant minuit.	We will be gone before midnight.

NOTE: The future perfect is also used to express probability or conjecture, referring to the past.

Il aura sans doute appelé.	He has probably called.
Elles seront sorties sans leurs chapeaux.	They probably went out without their hats.

The Past Conditional

The past conditional is formed with the conditional of *avoir* or *être* and a past participle.

ralentir I would have slowed down, etc.

j'aurais ralenti	nous aurions ralenti
tu aurais ralenti	vous auriez ralenti
il (elle, on) aurait ralenti	ils (elles) auraient ralenti

devenir I would have become, etc.

je serais devenu(e)	nous serions devenu(e)s
tu serais devenu(e)	vous seriez devenu(e)(s)
il (elle, on) serait devenu(e)	ils (elles) seraient devenu(e)s

J'aurais ralenti si j'avais vu l'agent de police.	I would have slowed down if I had seen the policeman.
Il serait mort d'asphyxie.	He would have died of asphyxiation.

NOTE: The conditional perfect is also used to express probability or conjecture, referring to the past.

Il aurait sans doute appelé.	He would probably have called.
Il serait peut-être arrivé à le faire.	He would perhaps have succeeded in doing it.

Perfect Tenses

Avoir Plus Past Participle

Passé Composé	ai + *past participle*	avons _____
	as _____	avez _____
	a _____	ont _____
Plus-que-parfait	avais _____	avions _____
	avais _____	aviez _____
	avait _____	avaient _____

Preterite Perfect	eus _____	eûmes _____
	eus _____	eûtes _____
	eut _____	eurent _____
Future Perfect	aurai _____	aurons _____
	auras _____	aurez _____
	aura _____	auront _____
Past Conditional	aurais _____	aurions _____
	aurais _____	auriez _____
	aurait _____	auraient _____

Être Plus Past Participle

Passé Composé	suis *past participle*	sommes _____
	es _____	êtes _____
	est _____	sont _____
Plus-que-parfait	étais _____	étions _____
	étais _____	étiez _____
	était _____	étaient _____
Preterite Perfect	fus _____	fûmes _____
	fus _____	fûtes _____
	fut _____	furent _____
Future Perfect	serai _____	serons _____
	seras _____	serez _____
	sera _____	seront _____
Past Conditional	serais _____	serions _____
	serais _____	seriez _____
	serait _____	seraient _____

Synopsis of the Perfect Tenses

parler - je

Passé Composé	j'ai parlé	I have spoken, I spoke
Pluperfect	j'avais parlé	I had spoken
Preterite Perfect	j'eus parlé	I had spoken
Future Perfect	j'aurai parlé	I will have spoken
Past Conditional	j'aurais parlé	I would have spoken

aller - je

Passé Composé	je suis allé(e)	I have gone, I went
Pluperfect	j'étais allé(e)	I had gone
Preterite Perfect	je fus allé(e)	I had gone
Future Perfect	je serai allé(e)	I will have gone
Past Conditional	je serais allé(e)	I would have gone

4. Pronominal Verbs

A pronominal verb is composed of a reflexive pronoun and a verb. Pronominal verbs are used frequently in French. The reflexive pronouns are *me, te, se, nous, vous, se.* The reflexive pronoun in the infinitive is *se.*

Reflexive Verbs

A reflexive verb is one in which the subject and the object of the verb represent the same person. That is, the subject acts upon itself.

s'habiller to get dressed

Present

I get dressed (dress myself), etc.

je m'habille	**nous nous habillons**
tu t'habilles	**vous vous habillez**
il (elle, on) s'habille	**ils (elles) s'habillent**

Je me lève à sept heures.	I get up at seven o'clock.
Nous nous préparons à sortir.	We are getting ready to go out.
Les garçons se promènent sur la plage.	The boys are walking on the beach.

NOTE: The negative *ne* always comes before the reflexive pronoun and *pas* after the verb.

Vous *ne* **vous arrêtez** *pas* à Lyon?	Aren't you stopping in Lyon?

With inversion, the reflexive pronoun precedes the verb.

Vous **reposez-vous?**	Are you resting?

Compound Tenses

All reflexive verbs take *être* as the auxiliary in compound tenses. The reflexive pronoun immediately precedes *être*, and the past participle agrees in number and gender with the subject.

Suzanne, à quelle heure t'es-tu levée ce matin?	Suzanne, at what time did you get up this morning?
Nos parents s'étaient dépêchés.	Our parents hurried up.
Mes cousines se seraient bien amusées.	My cousins would have enjoyed themselves.

NOTE: The negative *ne* always comes before the reflexive pronoun and *pas* after the auxiliary verb.

Ils *ne* se seront *pas* rencontrés avant midi.

They will not have met before noon.

Reciprocal Verbs

A reciprocal verb is used when the action passes from one person or thing to another, or from one group to another. It is only used in the first and third persons plural.

Nous nous sommes battus.
We fought each other.

Elles se sont entendues.
They got along together.

Some Verbs that Change Meaning When Used Pronominally

agir to act, to behave	**s'agir de** to be about
aller to go	**s'en aller** to go away
amuser to amuse (someone else)	**s'amuser** to enjoy oneself, to have a good time
appeler to call	**s'appeler** to be called, to be named
asseoir to seat	**s'asseoir** to sit down
battre to beat	**se battre** to fight
demander to ask	**se demander** to wonder
endormir to put to sleep	**s'endormir** to fall asleep
ennuyer to annoy	**s'ennuyer** to get bored
lever to raise, to lift	**se lever** to get up
passer to pass, to spend (time)	**se passer** to happen
	se passer de to do without
rappeler to call back	**se rappeler** to recall, to remember
retourner to return, to go back	**se retourner** to turn around
vanter to praise	**se vanter** to boast

NOTE: When a reflexive verb is used with a part of the body, there is no agreement of the past participle.

Il s'est lavé les dents.
He brushed his teeth.

Elle s'est cassé le cou.
She broke her neck.

5. Formation of Subjunctive Tenses

The subjunctive is the mood of uncertainty and emotion, and usually is used to reflect the speaker's attitude. The subjunctive occurs most frequently in dependent clauses introduced by *que*. (The varied uses of the subjunctive will be explained in Chapter 6.) There are four tenses of the subjunctive. The first two tenses are commonly used in everyday speech; the second two are used only in writing.

NOTE: The subjunctive forms of irregular verbs are included in Chapter 8.

Subjunctive Tenses

Present	Le présent
Past	Le passé
Imperfect	L'imparfait
Pluperfect	Le plus-que-parfait

Present Subjunctive

The regular present subjunctive is formed by adding the endings *-e, -es, -e, -ions, -iez, ent* to the *ils* (third person plural) form of the present indicative (drop the *-ent*).

parler

que je parle	que nous parlions		
que tu parles	que vous parliez		
qu'il (elle, on) parle	qu'ils (elles) parlent		

finir

que je finisse	que nous finissions
que tu finisses	que vous finissiez
qu'il (elle, on) finisse	qu'ils (elles) finissent

vendre

que je vende	que nous vendions
que tu vendes	que vous vendiez
qu'il (elle, on) vende	qu'ils (elles) vendent

Je voudrais que tu m'*aimes*.	I would like you to love me.
Il faut que vous *finissiez* vos lettres ce soir.	You must finish your letters tonight.
On ira dans ta voiture, à moins que tu ne la *vendes*.	We'll go in your car, unless you sell it.

Past Subjunctive

The past subjunctive is formed with the present subjunctive of *avoir* or *être* and the past participle of the verb.

parler, finir, vendre

que j'*aie* parlé (fini/vendu)
que tu *aies* parlé (fini/vendu)
qu'il (elle, on) *ait* parlé
  (fini/vendu)

que nous *ayons* parlé (fini/vendu)
que vous *ayez* parlé (fini/vendu)
qu'ils (elles) *aient* parlé (fini/vendu)

monter

que je *sois* monté(e)
que tu *sois* monté(e)
qu'il (elle, on) *soit* monté(e)

que nous *soyons* monté(e)s
que vous *soyez* monté(e)(s)
qu'ils (elles) *soient* monté(e)s

Je suis heureux que vous *ayez* aimé cette pièce.	I am happy that you liked that play.
C'est dommage qu'elle *soit* déjà partie.	It's a pity that she has already left.
Elle regrette que nous *ne soyons pas venus*.	She is sorry that we did not come.

Imperfect Subjunctive

The imperfect and the pluperfect of the subjunctive exist in classical literature. However, because of their cumbersome aspect, they are never used in spoken language. In modern literature, writers may still use the third person singular. Most of the time, however, the imperfect is replaced by the present subjunctive, and the pluperfect is replaced by the past subjunctive.

The imperfect subjunctive is formed with the *passé simple*. Drop the last letter of the first person singular and add the endings -*sse*, -*sses*, -^*t*, -*ssions*, -*ssiez*, -*ssent*. These endings are the same for all verbs.

parler

que je parla*sse*   que nous parla*ssions*
que tu parla*sses*   que vous parla*ssiez*
qu'il (elle, on)   qu'ils (elles)
  parlà*t*   parla*ssent*

finir

que je fini*sse*   que nous fini*ssions*
que tu fini*sses*   que vous fini*ssiez*
qu'il (elle, on)   qu'ils (elles)
  finì*t*   fini*ssent*

vendre

que je vendi*sse*   que nous vendi*ssions*
que tu vendi*sses*   que vous vendi*ssiez*
qu'il (elle, on) vendì*t* qu'ils (elles) vendi*ssent*

Il fallait qu'il vous *aimât* (aime) beaucoup pour faire cela.	He had to love you very much to do that.
Elle parlait fort pour qu'on n'*entendît* (entende) pas les cris de l'enfant.	She spoke loudly so that one could not hear the child crying.
Il insista pour que Marc *vendît* (vende) sa voiture.	He insisted that Marc sell his car.

Pluperfect Subjunctive

The pluperfect subjunctive is formed with the imperfect subjunctive of the auxiliary verbs *être* or *avoir* and the past participle.

parler, finir, vendre

que j'*eusse* parlé (fini/vendu)
que tu *eusses* parlé (fini/vendu)
qu'il (elle, on) *eût* parlé
    (fini/vendu)

que nous *eussions* parlé (fini/vendu)
que vous *eussiez* parlé (fini/vendu)
qu'ils (elles) *eussent* parlé
    (fini/vendu)

descendre

que je *fusse* descendu(e)
que tu *fusses* descendu(e)
qu'il (elle, on) *fût* descendu(e)

que nous *fussions* descendu(e)s
que vous *fussiez* descendu(e)(s)
qu'ils (elles) *fussent* descendu(e)s

Serait-il possible qu'il l'*eût*
    (ait) aimée plus que toutes les
    autres?
Nous n'avons pas pensé qu'il *fût*
    (soit) déjà arrivé.

Would it be possible that he had
    loved her more than all the
    others?
We did not think that he had
    already arrived.

Subjunctive Tenses

	-er		-ir		-re	
esent	___e	___ions	___isse	___issions	___e	___ions
	___es	___iez	___isses	___issiez	___es	___iez
	___e	___ent	___isse	___issent	___e	___ent
st	aie ___é	ayons ___é	aie ___i	ayons ___i	aie ___u	ayons ___u
	aies ___é	ayez ___é	aies ___i	ayez ___i	aies ___u	ayez ___u
	ait ___é	aient ___é	ait ___i	aient ___i	ait ___u	aient ___u
	sois ___é	soyons ___é	sois ___i	soyons ___i	sois ___u	soyons ___u
	sois ___é	soyez ___é	sois ___i	soyez ___i	sois ___u	soyez ___u
	soit ___é	soient ___é	soit ___i	soient ___i	soit ___u	soient ___u
perfect	___asse	___assions	___isse	___issions	___isse	___issions
	___asses	___assiez	___isses	___issiez	___isses	___issiez
	___ât	___assent	___ît	___issent	___ît	___issent
uperfect	eusse ___é	eussions ___é	eusse ___i	eussions ___i	eusse ___u	eussions ___u
	eusses ___é	eussiez ___é	eusses ___i	eussiez ___i	eusses ___u	eussiez ___u
	eût ___é	eussent ___é	eût ___i	eussent ___i	eût ___u	eussent ___u
	fusse ___é	fussions ___é	fusse ___i	fussions ___i	fusse ___u	fussions ___u
	fusses ___é	fussiez ___é	fusses ___i	fussiez ___i	fusses ___u	fussiez ___u
	fût ___é	fussent ___é	fût ___i	fussent ___i	fût ___u	fussent ___u

Verb Synopsis of Subjunctive Tenses

parler - il

Present	qu'il parle	he speaks
Past	qu'il ait parlé	he spoke
Imperfect	qu'il parlât	he spoke
Pluperfect	qu'il eût parlé	he had spoken

arriver - il

Present	qu'il arrive	he arrives
Past	qu'il soit arrivé	he arrived
Imperfect	qu'il arrivât	he arrived
Pluperfect	qu'il fût arrivé	he had arrived

6. Uses of the Subjunctive

Use of the Subjunctive in Main and Independent Clauses

In Commands

The subjunctive in the main clause or in an independent clause is used to express a command, a suggestion, a wish, or a regret. It is used most often in the third person.

Que personne ne sorte!	No one can go out!
Que Dieu vous entende!	May God hear you!
Ah! Qu'elle ne fût jamais partie!	If only she had never left!

In Fixed Expressions

The subjunctive is also used in some fixed expressions such as the following:

Vivent les vacances!	Hurray for vacations!
Dieu vous bénisse!	God bless you!
Sauve qui peut!	Every man for himself!
Advienne que pourra!	Come what may!
Ainsi soit-il!	So be it! Amen!
Honni soit qui mal y pense!	Evil be to him who evil thinks!

Use of the Subjunctive in Dependent Clauses

After Impersonal Expressions

1. Most impersonal expressions that convey the speaker's will, desire, or judgment are followed by the subjunctive. All impersonal expressions are followed by *que*. Below is a list of the most common impersonal expressions requiring the subjunctive.

il faut it is necessary	il est préférable it is preferable
il est bon it is good	il est peu probable it is hardly probable
il est mauvais it is bad	il arrive it happens
il est bien it is well	il vaut mieux it is better
il est possible it is possible	il suffit it is sufficient
il semble it seems	c'est dommage it is a pity
il est important it is important	peu importe never mind
il est utile it is useful	nul doute no doubt
il est temps it is time	il se peut it may be
il est impossible it is impossible	

Il arrive que nous soyons absents l'après-midi.	It happens that we are absent in the afternoon.
Il faut que vous obéissiez à vos parents.	It is necessary for you to obey your parents.
Il se peut qu'ils aillent en France.	It may be that they are going to France.
Nul doute que tu aies l'intention de te marier.	No doubt you intend to marry.

2.   Impersonal expressions that introduce a fact or certainty are followed by the indicative. Some of those expressions include:

il est certain	it is certain	il est probable	it is probable
il est évident	it is evident	il est vrai	it is true
il me semble	it seems to me	il paraît	it seems

Il est certain que l'hiver est arrivé.	It is certain that winter has come.
Il est évident que Paul ne reviendra pas.	It is evident that Paul will not come back.
Il est probable que nous avons trop mangé.	It is probable that we have eaten too much.

3.   If the impersonal expressions indicating certainty are used in the negative in the main clause, the subjunctive is used in the dependent clause.

Il n'est pas vrai que les Français soient tous petits.	It is not true that the French are all short.
Il ne semble pas que vous ayez beaucoup travaillé.	It does not seem that you have worked much.

After Verbs of Volition

The subjunctive is used in dependent clauses after verbs expressing the speaker's mind or will: desire, judgment, command, or forbidding. The subjunctive is used in the dependent clause only when each clause has a different subject. If there is only one subject, an infinitive is used. Here is a partial list of verbs of volition:

aimer mieux } préférer }	to prefer	exiger to demand, to require
		tenir à ce (que) to insist
souhaiter to wish		vouloir to want, to wish
permettre to allow, to permit		défendre to forbid
conseiller to advise		demander to ask
ordonner to command		prier to pray, to beg
dire to tell		compter to expect

Ma mère me défend de sortir tard.	My mother forbids me to go out late.
Ma mère défend que nous sortions tard.	My mother forbids us to go out late.
J'exige que tu mettes de l'argent de côté.	I demand that you save money.
Ton père souhaite que tu n'oublies pas de lui écrire.	Your father wishes you not to forget to write him.
Elle veut que je fasse le ménage.	She wants me to do the housework.

After Verbs of Emotion

The subjunctive is also used after expressions of emotion (joy, fear, sorrow, regret, surprise).

avoir peur (...ne) to be afraid	**être surpris** to be surprised
être content to be glad, to be pleased	**se réjouir** to rejoice
être désolé to be sorry	**se plaindre** to complain
être enchanté to be delighted	**s'étonner** to be astonished
être heureux to be happy	**regretter** to regret
être malheureux to be unhappy	**craindre (...ne)** to fear

Je suis enchanté que vous ayez pu venir.	I am delighted that you could come.
Je m'étonne que vous travailliez si tard.	I am surprised that you are working so late.

NOTE: Some verbs, like *avoir peur* and *craindre,* call for *ne* in the subjunctive clause (without the effect of a negative), if the sentence is a declarative affirmative sentence. In negative and interrogative sentences the *ne* is omitted.

Craignez-vous qu'il soit malade?	Do you fear that he is sick?
Non, je crains qu'il *ne* mente.	No, I fear that he is lying.

After Verbs of Doubt and Denial

The subjunctive is also used after expressions of doubt and denial, when the speaker wants to convey the possibility of something in his mind, if not in reality.

douter to doubt	**croire** to believe, to think
ne pas être sûr to not be sure	**penser** to think
ne pas être certain to not be certain	**espérer** to hope

The verbs *croire, penser,* and *espérer* take the subjunctive only in negative and interrogative sentences.

Je ne suis pas sûre qu'elle ait pris son parapluie.	I am not sure that she has taken her umbrella.
Croyez-vous qu'elle soit malade?	Do you think she is sick?
Non, je crois qu'elle va bien.	No, I believe she is well.

After Conjunctions

The subjunctive is always used after the following conjunctions:

Time	Condition
avant que (...ne) before	**à moins que(...ne)** unless
en attendant que while waiting	**pourvu que** provided that, hopefully
jusqu'à ce que until	**sans que** without

Goal		Others	
pour que in order that		bien que ⎫ although	
afin que so that		quoique ⎭	
de manière que ⎫ so that		malgré que despite the fact	
de façon que ⎭		puisque since	
		soit que...soit que either that...or that	
Emotion		qui que whoever	
de peur que (...ne) for fear that,		quoi que whatever	
de crainte que (...ne) lest			

Qui que vous soyez, ouvrez la porte!	Whoever you are, open the door!
Nous irons à la plage, à moins qu'il ne pleuve.	We will go to the beach unless it rains.
Pourvu qu'il ne neige pas!	Hopefully, it will not snow!

In Relative Clauses

1.   The subjunctive is used in a relative clause when the antecedent is a superlative or one of these adjectives: *seul, premier, dernier, unique, suprême.*

C'est la plus belle ville que j'aie jamais vue.	It is the most beautiful city I have ever seen.
C'est la seule langue que je connaisse.	It's the only language I know.

2.   The subjunctive also comes after certain negatives: *rien, peu de, pas un, ne rien, ne personne.*

Je ne sais rien qui vaille la peine d'être répété.	I don't know anything that is worth repeating.
Il y a peu de chance qu'il réussisse.	There is little chance he will succeed.

3.   When the sentence expresses a goal, an intention, or a consequence, the relative clause takes the subjunctive.

Je cherche quelqu'un qui parle chinois.	I am looking for someone who speaks Chinese.
Il n'y a personne qui puisse m'aider.	There is no one who could help me.

7. Orthographic-Changing Verbs

Orthographic-changing verbs are those verbs that change spelling in some forms in order to preserve a vowel or consonant sound.

1. Verbs whose infinitives end in -cer change the c to ç before a and o to retain the soft c sound.

commencer to begin, to start *commençant* *commencé* (aux. *avoir*)

> Pres. je commence, tu commences, il commence, **nous commençons**, vous commencez, ils commencent
>
> Imper. **je commençais, tu commençais, il commençait,** nous commencions, vous commenciez, **ils commençaient**
>
> Passé Simple **je commençai, tu commenças, il commença, nous commençâmes, vous commençâtes,** ils commencèrent

Other verbs of this type:

annoncer to announce	**menacer** to threaten
avancer to advance, to be fast (a watch)	**placer** to place, to set
	prononcer to pronounce
effacer to erase	**remplacer** to replace
exercer to exercise	**renoncer à** to give up
lancer to throw	

2. Verbs whose infinitives end in -ger add an e after g before a or o to retain the soft g sound.

manger to eat *mangeant* *mangé* (aux. *avoir*)

> Pres. je mange, tu manges, il mange, **nous mangeons**, vous mangez, ils mangent
>
> Imper. **je mangeais, tu mangeais, il mangeait,** nous mangions, vous mangiez, **ils mangeaient**
>
> Passé Simple **je mangeai, tu mangeas, il mangea, nous mangeâmes, vous mangeâtes,** ils mangèrent

Other verbs of this type:

arranger to put in order	**neiger** to snow
bouger to move	**obliger** to oblige
changer to change	**partager** to share
corriger to correct	**plonger** to dive, to plunge
déranger to disturb	**protéger** to protect
exiger to require	**songer** to imagine
infliger to inflict	**soulager** to ease (pain)
nager to swim	**voyager** to travel

3.   Verbs with infinitives ending in -*yer* change the *y* to an *i* before a mute *e*.

employer to use, to employ   *employant*   *employé* (aux. *avoir*)

Pres.   **j'emploie, tu emploies, il emploie**, nous employons, vous employez, **ils
emploient**

Fut.   **j'emploierai, tu emploieras, il emploiera, nous emploierons, vous
emploierez, ils emploieront**

Cond.   **j'emploierais, tu emploierais, il emploierait, nous emploierions, vous
emploieriez, ils emploieraient**

NOTE: Verbs ending in -*ayer* may keep the *y* or change to *i*: *il paye* or *il paie*.

Other verbs of this type:

balayer to sweep	**nettoyer** to clean
ennuyer to bore	**se noyer** to drown
essayer to try	**payer** to pay
essuyer to wipe	

4. Verbs containing a mute *e* in the last syllable before the infinitive ending
change the mute *e* to an *è* if the next syllable contains a mute *e*.

acheter to buy   *achetant*   *acheté* (aux. *avoir*)

Pres.   **j'achète, tu achètes, il achète**, nous achetons, vous achetez, **ils achètent**

Fut.   **j'achèterai, tu achèteras, il achètera, nous achèterons, vous achèterez, ils
achèteront**

Cond.   **j'achèterais, tu achèterais, il achèterait, nous achèterions, vous
achèteriez, ils achèteraient**

Other verbs of this type:

achever to complete	**se lever** to get up
élever to raise, to bring up	**mener** to lead (someone)
emmener to take away (someone)	**peser** to weigh
lever to raise	**se promener** to take a walk

5.   Verbs with infinitives ending in -*eler* and -*eter* double the *l* or *t*.

jeter to throw (away)   *jetant*   *jeté* (aux. *avoir*)

Pres.   **je jette, tu jettes, il jette**, nous jetons, vous jetez, **ils jettent**

Fut.   **je jetterai, tu jetteras, il jettera, nous jetterons, vous jetterez, ils jetteront**

Cond.   **je jetterais, tu jetterais, il jetterait, nous jetterions, vous jetteriez, ils
jetteraient**

Other verbs of this type:

appeler to call	**rappeler** to call again
s'appeler to be named	**se rappeler** to recall

6.   Verbs with *é* in the next to last syllable of the infinitive change the *é* to *è*
if the *e* is the last pronounced vowel.

préférer to prefer   *préférant*   *préféré* (aux. *avoir*)

Pres.   **je préfère, tu préfères, il préfère**, nous préférons, vous préférez, **ils
préfèrent**

Other verbs of this type:

céder to yield	**interpréter** to interpret
célébrer to celebrate	**posséder** to possess
compléter to complete	**protéger** to protect
espérer to hope	**répéter** to repeat
exagérer to exaggerate	**révéler** to reveal

NOTE: The verb *créer* ("to create") retains the *é* in all forms.

8. Irregular Verbs

In this chapter, only the irregular tenses are given; you may assume that the remaining tenses of the verbs are regular. Check regular tense formation in Chapter 2 (simple tenses), Chapter 3 (perfect tenses), and Chapter 5 (subjunctive mood). Present and past participles are given.

Auxiliary Verbs

avoir to have *ayant* *eu* (aux. *avoir*)

> Pres.   j'ai, tu as, il a, nous avons, vous avez, ils ont
> Fut.   j'aurai, tu auras, il aura, nous aurons, vous aurez, ils auront
> Pres. Subj.   j'aie, tu aies, il ait, nous ayons, vous ayez, ils aient
> Passé Simple   j'eus, tu eus, il eut, nous eûmes, vous eûtes, ils eurent
> Imperative   aie, ayons, ayez

être to be *étant* *été* (aux. *avoir*)

> Pres.   je suis, tu es, il est, nous sommes, vous êtes, ils sont
> Imper.   j'étais, tu étais, il était, nous étions, vous étiez, ils étaient
> Fut.   je serai, tu seras, il sera, nous serons, vous serez, ils seront
> Pres. Subj.   je sois, tu sois, il soit, nous soyons, vous soyez, ils soient
> Passé Simple   je fus, tu fus, il fut, nous fûmes, vous fûtes, il furent
> Imperative   sois, soyons, soyez

Other Irregular Verbs

absoudre to absolve, to forgive *absolvant* *absous* (aux. *avoir*)

> Pres.   j'absous, tu absous, il absout, nous absolvons, vous absolvez, ils absolvent

Other verbs of this type:

dissoudre to dissolve

acquérir to acquire *acquérant* *acquis* (aux. *avoir*)

> Pres.   j'acquiers, tu acquiers, il acquiert, nous acquérons, vous acquérez, ils acquièrent
> Fut.   j'acquerrai, tu acquerras, il acquerra, nous acquerrons, vous acquerrez, ils acquerront
> Passé Simple   j'acquis, tu acquis, il acquit, nous acquîmes, vous acquîtes, ils acquirent

Other verbs of this type:

conquérir to conquer
requérir to ask for

aller to go   *allant*   *allé* (aux. *être*)

  Pres. je vais, tu vas, il va, nous allons, vous allez, ils vont
  Fut. j'irai, tu iras, il ira, nous irons, vous irez, ils iront
  Pres. Subj. j'aille, tu ailles, il aille, nous allions, vous alliez, ils aillent

Other verbs of this type:

s'en aller to go away (aux. *être*)

assaillir to assail   *assaillant*   *assailli* (aux. *avoir*)

  Pres. j'assaille, tu assailles, il assaille, nous assaillons, vous assaillez, ils assaillent

Other verbs of this type:

défaillir to become feeble

asseoir to seat   *asseyant*   *assis* (aux. *avoir*)

  Pres. j'assieds, tu assieds, il assied, nous asseyons, vous asseyez, ils asseyent
  Fut. j'assiérai, tu assiéras, il assiéra, nous assiérons, vous assiérez, ils assiéront
  Passé Simple j'assis, tu assis, il assit, nous assîmes, vous assîtes, ils assirent

Other verbs of this type:

s'asseoir to sit down (aux. *être*)
(se rasseoir to sit down again)

battre to beat   *battant*   *battu* (aux. *avoir*)

  Pres. je bats, tu bats, il bat, nous battons, vous battez, ils battent

Other verbs of this type:

abattre to knock down	**débattre** to debate
combattre to battle with	**se battre** to fight

boire to drink   *buvant*   *bu* (aux. *avoir*)

  Pres. je bois, tu bois, il boit, nous buvons, vous buvez, ils boivent
  Passé Simple je bus, tu bus, il but, nous bûmes, vous bûtes, ils burent

bouillir to boil   *bouillant*   *bouilli* (aux. *avoir*)

  Pres. je bous, tu bous, il bout, nous bouillons, vous bouillez, ils bouillent

conclure to conclude   *concluant*   *conclu* (aux. *avoir*)

  Pres. je conclus, tu conclus, il conclut, nous concluons, vous concluez, ils concluent
  Passé Simple je conclus, tu conclus, il conclut, nous conclûmes, vous conclûtes, ils conclurent

Other verbs of this type:

exclure to exclude
inclure to include

conduire to drive   *conduisant*   *conduit* (aux. *avoir*)

  Pres. je conduis, tu conduis, il conduit, nous conduisons, vous conduisez, ils conduisent
  Passé Simple je conduisis, tu conduisis, il conduisit, nous conduisîmes, vous conduisites, ils conduisirent

Other verbs of this type:

construire to build	**luire** to light up
cuire to cook	**nuire** to be hurtful
déduire to deduct	**produire** to produce
détruire to destruct	**réduire** to reduce
instruire to instruct	**reproduire** to reproduce
introduire to introduce	**traduire** to translate

connaître to know   *connaissant*   *connu* (aux. *avoir*)

Pres. **je connais, tu connais, il connaît, nous connaissons, vous connaissez, ils connaissent**
Passé Simple **je connus, tu connus, il connut, nous connûmes, vous connûtes, ils connurent**

Other verbs of this type:

apparaître to appear	**paraître** to seem, to appear
disparaître to disappear	**reconnaître** to recognize

coudre to sew   *cousant*   *cousu* (aux. *avoir*)

Pres. **je couds, tu couds, il coud, nous cousons, vous cousez, ils cousent**

courir to run   *courant*   *couru* (aux. *avoir*)

Pres. **je cours, tu cours, il court, nous courons, vous courez, ils courent**
Fut. **je courrai, tu courras, il courra, nous courrons, vous courrez, ils courront**

Other verbs of this type:

accourir to come running	**parcourir** to travel through
concourir to compete	**recourir** to resort
discourir to discourse	**secourir** to help, to come to
encourir to incur	the help of

craindre to fear   *craignant*   *craint* (aux. *avoir*)

Pres. **je crains, tu crains, il craint, nous craignons, vous craignez, ils craignent**
Passé Simple **je craignis, tu craignis, il craignit, nous craignîmes, vous craignîtes, ils craignirent**

Other verbs of this type:

atteindre to attain	**feindre** to feign, to simulate
dépeindre to depict	**joindre** to join
enceindre to surround	**peindre** to paint
enfeindre to infringe	**restreindre** to restrain
éteindre to extinguish	**teindre** to dye
étreindre to embrace	

croire to believe   *croyant*   *cru* (aux. *avoir*)

Pres. **je crois, tu crois, il croit, nous croyons, vous croyez, ils croient**
Passé Simple **je crus, tu crus, il crut, nous crûmes, vous crûtes, ils crurent**

croître to grow   *croissant*   *crû* (aux. *avoir*)

Pres. **je crois, tu crois, il croît, nous croissons, vous croissez, ils croissent**
Passé Simple **je crûs, tu crûs, il crût, nous crûmes, vous crûtes, ils crûrent**

Other verbs of this type:

accroître to increase
décroître to decrease

cueillir to pick (fruits and flowers)   *cueillant*   *cueilli* (aux. *avoir*)

Pres. **je cueille, tu cueilles, il cueille, nous cueillons, vous cueillez, ils cueillent**
Fut. **je cueillerai, tu cueilleras, il cueillera, nous cueillerons, vous cueillerez, ils cueilleront**

Other verbs of this type:

accueillir to welcome
recueillir to gather
se recueillir to collect one's thoughts

devoir must, to have to, should, to owe   *devant*   *dû* (aux. *avoir*)

Pres. **je dois, tu dois, il doit, nous devons, vous devez, ils doivent**
Pres. Subj. **je doive, tu doives, il doive, nous devions, vous deviez, ils doivent**
Passé Simple **je dus, tu dus, il dut, nous dûmes, vous dûtes, ils durent**

dire to say, to tell   *disant*   *dit* (aux. *avoir*)

Pres. **je dis, tu dis, il dit, nous disons, vous dites, ils disent**

Other verbs of this type:

contredire to contradict   **médire** to speak ill of
interdire to forbid   **prédire** to predict
maudire to curse

These have the ending -*isez* in the second person plural, except for *maudire*, with endings -*issons* and -*issez* in the first and second persons plural.

dormir to sleep   *dormant*   *dormi* (aux. *avoir*)

Pres. **je dors, tu dors, il dort, nous dormons, vous dormez, ils dorment**

Other verbs of this type:

endormir to put to sleep   **rendormir** to put back to sleep
s'endormir to go to sleep   **se rendormir** to go back to sleep

écrire to write   *écrivant*   *écrit* (aux. *avoir*)

Pres. **j'écris, tu écris, il écrit, nous écrivons, vous écrivez, ils écrivent**
Passé Simple **j'écrivis, tu écrivis, il écrivit, nous écrivîmes, vous écrivîtes, ils écrivirent**

Other verbs of this type:

décrire to describe   **souscrire** to subscribe
s'inscrire to register   **transcrire** to transcribe

envoyer to send   *envoyant*   *envoyé* (aux. *avoir*)

(See also Orthographic-Changing Verbs.)
Fut. **j'enverrai, tu enverras, il enverra, nous enverrons, vous enverrez, ils enverront**

Other verbs of this type:

renvoyer to send back, to fire (someone)

faillir to nearly do (something), to fail   *faillant*   *failli* (aux. *avoir*)

This verb is used only in the infinitive, passé simple, future, conditional, and perfect tenses.

Fut.   **je faillirai, tu failliras, il faillira, nous faillirons, vous faillirez, ils failliront**
Passé Simple   **je faillis, tu faillis, il faillit, nous faillîmes, vous faillîtes, ils faillirent**

faire to do, to make   *faisant*   *fait* (aux. *avoir*)

Pres.   **je fais, tu fais, il fait, nous faisons, vous faites, ils font**
Fut.   **je ferai, tu feras, il fera, nous ferons, vous ferez, ils feront**
Passé Simple   **je fis, tu fis, il fit, nous fîmes, vous fîtes, ils firent**

Other verbs of this type:

contrefaire to counterfeit	**refaire** to redo
défaire to undo	**satisfaire** to satisfy
parfaire to perfect	**surfaire** to overestimate

fuir to flee   *fuyant*   *fui* (aux. *avoir*)

Pres.   **je fuis, tu fuis, il fuit, nous fuyons, vous fuyez, ils fuient**

Other verbs of this type:

s'enfuir to flee

lire to read   *lisant*   *lu* (aux. *avoir*)

Pres.   **je lis, tu lis, il lit, nous lisons, vous lisez, ils lisent**
Passé Simple   **je lus, tu lus, il lut, nous lûmes, vous lûtes, ils lurent**

Other verbs of this type:

élire to elect	**relire** to reread
réélire to reelect	

mettre to put   *mettant*   *mis* (aux. *avoir*)

Pres.   **je mets, tu mets, il met, nous mettons, vous mettez, ils mettent**

Other verbs of this type:

admettre to admit	**permettre** to permit
commettre to commit	**remettre** to postpone
compromettre to compromise	**soumettre** to submit
émettre to emit	**transmettre** to transmit
omettre to omit	

moudre to grind   *moulant*   *moulu* (aux. *avoir*)

Pres.   **je mouds, tu mouds, il moud, nous moulons, vous moulez, ils moulent**
Passé Simple   **je moulus, tu moulus, il moulut, nous moulûmes, vous moulûtes, ils moulurent**

Other verbs of this type:

émoudre to sharpen

mourir to die   *mourant*   *mort* (aux. *être*)

Pres. **je meurs, tu meurs, il meurt, nous mourons, vous mourez, ils meurent**
Fut. **je mourrai, tu mourras, il mourra, nous mourrons, vous mourrez, ils mourront**
Passé Simple **je mourus, tu mourus, il mourut, nous mourûmes, vous mourûtes, il moururent**

mouvoir to move   *mouvant*   *mu* (aux. *avoir*)

Pres. **je meus, tu meus, il meut, nous mouvons, vous mouvez, ils meuvent**
Passé Simple **je mus, tu mus, il mut, nous mûmes, vous mûtes, ils murent**

Other verbs of this type:

émouvoir to move, to touch
s'émouvoir to be moved
promouvoir to promote

naître to be born   *naissant*   *né* (aux. *être*)

Pres. **je nais, tu nais, il naît, nous naissons, vous naissez, ils naissent**
Passé Simple **je naquis, tu naquis, il naquit, nous naquîmes, vous naquîtes, ils naquirent**

ouvrir to open   *ouvrant*   *ouvert* (aux. *avoir*)

Pres. **j'ouvre, tu ouvres, il ouvre, nous ouvrons, vous ouvrez, ils ouvrent**
Passé Simple **j'ouvris, tu ouvris, il ouvrit, nous ouvrîmes, vous ouvrîtes, ils ouvrirent**

Other verbs of this type:

couvrir to cover	**recouvrir** to recover
découvrir to discover	**rouvrir** to reopen
offrir to offer	**souffrir** to suffer

partir to leave   *partant*   *parti* (aux. *être*)

Pres. **je pars, tu pars, il part, nous partons, vous partez, ils partent**

Other verbs of this type:

départir to assign, to accord	**repartir** to leave again
se départir to abandon	**répartir** to distribute

plaire to please   *plaisant*   *plu* (aux. *avoir*)

Pres. **je plais, tu plais, il plaît, nous plaisons, vous plaisez, ils plaisent**
Passé Simple **je plus, tu plus, il plut, nous plûmes, vous plûtes, ils plurent**

Other verbs of this type:

déplaire to displease

pourvoir to provide   *pourvoyant*   *pourvu* (aux. *avoir*)

Pres. **je pourvois, tu pourvois, il pourvoit, nous pourvoyons, vous pourvoyez, ils pourvoient**
Fut. **je pourvoirai, tu pourvoiras, il pourvoira, nous pourvoirons, vous pourvoirez, ils pourvoiront**

pouvoir to be able to, can, may   *pouvant*   *pu* (aux. *avoir*)

Pres.   je peux, tu peux, il peut, nous pouvons, vous pouvez, il peuvent
Fut.   je pourrai, tu pourras, il pourra, nous pourrons, vous pourrez, ils pourront
Pres. Subj.   je puisse, tu puisses, il puisse, nous puissions, vous puissiez, ils puissent

prendre to take   *prenant*   *pris* (aux. *avoir*)

Pres.   je prends, tu prends, il prend, nous prenons, vous prenez, ils prennent
Pres. Subj.   je prenne, tu prennes, il prenne, nous prenions, vous preniez, ils prennent
Passé Simple   je pris, tu pris, il prit, nous prîmes, vous prîtes, ils prirent

Other verbs of this type:

apprendre to learn	**se méprendre** to be mistaken
comprendre to understand	**reprendre** to take back
entreprendre to undertake	**surprendre** to surprise

résoudre to resolve, to determine   *résolvant*   *résolu* (determined) (aux. *avoir*)
                                                   résous (resolved)

Pres.   je résous, tu résous, il résout, nous résolvons, vous résolvez, ils résolvent
Passé Simple   je résolus, tu résolus, il résolut, nous résolûmes, vous résolûtes, ils résolurent

rire to laugh   *riant*   *ri* (aux. *avoir*)

Pres.   je ris, tu ris, il rit, nous rions, vous riez, ils rient

Other verbs of this type:

se rire de to laugh at
sourire to smile

savoir to know, to know how   *sachant*   *su* (aux. *avoir*)

Pres.   je sais, tu sais, il sait, nous savons, vous savez, ils savent
Fut.   je saurai, tu sauras, il saura, nous saurons, vous saurez, ils sauront
Pres. Subj.   je sache, tu saches, il sache, nous sachions, vous sachiez, ils sachent
Imperative   sache, sachons, sachez

sentir to feel, to smell   *sentant*   *senti* (aux. *avoir*)

Pres.   je sens, tu sens, il sent, nous sentons, vous sentez, ils sentent

Other verbs of this type:

consentir to consent	**ressentir** to feel pain, emotion
démentir to deny	**se sentir** to feel
mentir to lie	**se repentir** to repent, rue

servir to serve   *servant*   *servi* (aux. *avoir*)

Pres.   je sers, tu sers, il sert, nous servons, vous servez, ils servent

Other verbs of this type:

se servir de to use, to make use of

sortir to go out   *sortant*   *sorti* (aux. *être*)

Pres.   je sors, tu sors, il sort, nous sortons, vous sortez, ils sortent *suffire* to suffice, to be sufficient   *suffisant*   *suffi* (aux. *avoir*)

    Pres. **je suffis, tu suffis, il suffit, nous suffisons, vous suffisez, ils suffisent**

    Other verbs of this type:

    se suffire to be self-sufficient

suivre to follow   *suivant*   *suivi* (aux. *avoir*)

    Pres. **je suis, tu suis, il suit, nous suivons, vous suivez, ils suivent**

    Other verbs of this type:

    poursuivre to pursue

taire to say nothing   *taisant*   *tu* (aux. *avoir*)

    Pres. **je tais, tu tais, il tait, nous taisons, vous taisez, ils taisent**
    Passé Simple **je tus, tu tus, il tut, nous tûmes, vous tûtes, ils turent**

    Other verbs of this type:

    se taire to be quiet, to hold one's tongue

traire to milk (a cow)   *trayant*   *trait* (aux. *avoir*)

    Pres. **je trais, tu trais, il trait, nous trayons, vous trayez, ils traient**

This verb has no *passé simple* or imperfect subjunctive forms.

    Other verbs of this type:

abstraire to abstract	**extraire** to extract
distraire to distract	**soustraire** to subtract

vaincre to conquer   *vainquant*   *vaincu* (aux. *avoir*)

    Pres. **je vaincs, tu vaincs, il vainc, nous vainquons, vous vainquez, ils vainquent**
    Passé Simple **je vainquis, tu vainquis, il vainquit, nous vainquîmes, vous vainquîtes, ils vainquirent**

    Other verbs of this type:

    convaincre to convince
    se convaincre to convince oneself

valoir to be worth   *valant*   *valu* (aux. *avoir*)

    Pres. **je vaux, tu vaux, il vaut, nous valons, vous valez, ils valent**
    Fut. **je vaudrai, tu vaudras, il vaudra, nous vaudrons, vous vaudrez, ils vaudront**
    Pres. Subj. **je vaille, tu vailles, il vaille, nous valions, vous valiez, ils vaillent**

venir to come   *venant*   *venu* (aux. *être*)

    Pres. **je viens, tu viens, il vient, nous venons, vous venez, ils viennent**
    Fut. **je viendrai, tu viendras, il viendra, nous viendrons, vous viendrez, ils viendront**
    Passé Simple **je vins, tu vins, il vint, nous vînmes, vous vîntes, ils vinrent**

Other verbs of this type:
(with *avoir* as the auxiliary)

appartenir à to belong to	**prévenir** to warn
contenir to contain	**retenir** to hold back
convenir à to suit, to be suitable	**soutenir** to support
détenir to hold, to detain	**subvenir** to provide for
intervenir to intervene	**survenir** to happen unexpectedly
maintenir to maintain	**tenir** to hold
obtenir to obtain	

(with *être* as the auxiliary)

se convenir to agree with each other	**revenir** to come back
devenir to become	**se souvenir de** to remember
parvenir to attain, succeed (in)	**se tenir** to remain, to keep

vêtir to clothe   *vêtant*   *vêtu*   (aux. *avoir*)

Pres. **je vêts, tu vêts, il vêt, nous vêtons, vous vêtez, ils vêtent**
Passé Simple **je vêtis, tu vêtis, il vêtit, nous vêtîmes, vous vêtîtes, ils vêtirent**

Other verbs of this type:

se vêtir to clothe oneself

vivre to live   *vivant*   *vécu*   (aux. *avoir*)

Pres. **je vis, tu vis, il vit, nous vivons, vous vivez, ils vivent**
Passé Simple **je vécus, tu vécus, il vécut, nous vécûmes, vous vécûtes, ils vécurent**

Other verbs of this type:

survivre to survive

voir to see   *voyant*   *vu*   (aux. *avoir*)

Pres. **je vois, tu vois, il voit, nous voyons, vous voyez, ils voient**
Fut. **je verrai, tu verras, il verra, nous verrons, vous verrez, ils verront**
Passé Simple **je vis, tu vis, il vit, nous vîmes, vous vîtes, ils virent**

Other verbs of this type:

apercevoir to have a glimpse of	**prévoir** to foresee (Fut.:
s'apercevoir to realize	*je prévoirai*, etc.)

vouloir to want, to wish   *voulant*   *voulu*   (aux. *avoir*)

Pres. **je veux, tu veux, il veut, nous voulons, vous voulez, ils veulent**
Fut. **je voudrai, tu voudras, il voudra, nous voudrons, vous voudrez, ils voudront**
Pres. Subj. **je veuille, tu veuilles, il veuille, nous voulions, vous vouliez, ils veuillent**
Imperative **veuille, veuillons, veuillez**

Other verbs of this type:

en vouloir à to bear ill will

9. Impersonal Verbs

Impersonal verbs are those that are used only in the third person singular with no definite subject.

Il y a

The expression *il y a* ("there is," "there are") implies existence. *Il y a* is used in any tense.

Il y a des fleurs sur la table.	There are flowers on the table.
Hier, il y avait beaucoup de fruits dans le jardin.	Yesterday, there was a lot of fruit in the garden.
C'est dommage qu'il y ait tant de monde.	It's too bad there are so many people.
Il n'y avait rien qui lui fasse peur.	There was nothing that frightened him.

Il y a is used in several common idiomatic expressions.

Qu'est-ce qu'il y a?	What's the matter?
Il y a quelque chose qui ne va pas.	There is something the matter.
Merci. Il n'y a pas de quoi.	Thank you. Don't mention it.
Il n'y a pas moyen d'être tranquille ici?	Could we have some quiet here?
Il y en a qui disent que la guerre va arriver.	There are some people who say that there will be a war.

Il y a is also used to express "ago," "for," and "since."

Je suis partie il y a un mois.	I left a month ago.
Il y a deux heures que je l'attends.	I have been waiting for him for two hours.
Il y a longtemps que je ne t'ai vu.	It's been a long time since I saw you.

Falloir

Falloir, "to be necessary," is one of the most commonly used impersonal verbs.

The forms of *falloir* most commonly used are: Present: **il faut**; Imperfect: **il fallait**; Passé Simple: **il fallut**; Future: **il faudra**; Conditional: **il faudrait**; Passé Composé: **il a fallu**; Pluperfect: **il avait fallu**; Future Perfect: **il aura fallu**; Past Conditional: **il aurait fallu**; Present Subjunctive: **il faille**.

Falloir is followed by the subjunctive or an infinitive.

Il faudrait que nous fassions la vaisselle.	It would be necessary for us to do the dishes.
Il a fallu qu'il prenne son billet un mois à l'avance.	He had to buy his ticket a month in advance.
Il faut manger pour vivre.	One must eat to live.
Il me faut des poireaux et des carottes pour la soupe.	I need leeks and carrots for the soup.

Idiomatic uses of *falloir:*

Mets le couvert comme il faut.	Set the table properly.
C'est plus qu'il n'en faut.	That's more than enough.
Voilà l'homme qu'il nous faut.	He's the very man we need.
Il s'en faut de beaucoup.	Not by a long shot.

Weather Expressions

bruiner	**il bruine**	it's drizzling
geler	**il gèle**	it's freezing

Two other verbs are conjugated like *geler: dégeler,* "to thaw," and *regeler,* "to freeze again." See Orthographic-Changing Verbs, Chapter 7.

grêler	**il grêle**	it's hailing

A verb conjugated like *grêler* is *regrêler,* "to hail again."

neiger	**il neige**	it's snowing

(See Orthographic-Changing Verbs, Chapter 7.) *Reneiger,* "to snow again," is conjugated like *neiger.*

pleuvoir	**il pleut**	it's raining

Other forms of *pleuvoir* are: Imperfect: **il pleuvait**; Passé Simple: **il plut**; Future: **il pleuvra**; Conditional: **il pleuvrait**; Past Participle: **plu**; Present Participle: **pleuvant**; Present Subjunctive: **il pleuve**. *Repleuvoir,* "to rain again," is conjugated like *pleuvoir.*

tonner	**il tonne**	it's thundering

Il ne cessa de bruiner.	It was drizzling constantly.
On gèle ici!	It's freezing here!
Il a grêlé pendant au moins un quart d'heure.	Hail fell for at least a quarter of an hour.
J'espère qu'il va neiger pour Noël.	I hope it snows at Christmas time.
Il pleut des cordes.	It's pouring.
Il a tonné pendant l'orage.	There was thunder during the storm.

Weather Expressions with *Faire*

Il fait beau.	The weather is beautiful.	Il fait mauvais.	The weather is bad.
Il fait chaud.	It's warm (hot).	Il fait sombre.	It's dark.
Il fait frais.	It's chilly.	Il fait du brouillard.	It's foggy.
Il fait froid.	It's cold.	Il fait de la brume.	It's hazy (misty).
Il fait lourd.	It's muggy.	Il fait de l'orage.	It's stormy.
Il fait du soleil.	It's sunny.	Il fait du vent.	It's windy.

NOTE: For more information on impersonal verbs and expressions, see Chapter 6, Uses of the Subjunctive.

10. Sequence of Tenses

The action expressed in a dependent clause can be simultaneous to, can precede, or can follow the action expressed in the main clause. This is true of sentences in the indicative mood, conditional sentences, and sentences calling for the subjunctive.

Tenses of the Indicative

Past Time					Present Time	Future Time	
	Imperfect						
Passé Simple		Passé Surcomposé					
Pluperfect	Preterite Perfect	Passé Composé	Future Perfect of the Past	Future of the Past	Present	Future Perfect	Future

The above chart shows a sequence of tenses in time. The tense most removed in past time is the pluperfect (*plus-que-parfait*); the farthest in the future is the future.

1. The *passé surcomposé* is formed by adding the *passé composé* of *être* or *avoir* to the past participle of the verb. It is mostly used after conjunctions of time: *quand, lorsque, dès que, aussitôt que.*

Dès qu'elle *a été aimée* pour elle-même, elle a guéri.	As soon as she was loved for herself, she was cured.
Quand j'*ai eu fini*, il a été convaincu.	When I finished, he was convinced.

2. The future perfect of the past (*futur antérieur du passé*) has the same forms as the past conditional.

J'étais sûre qu'il *aurait oublié* son parapluie.	I was sure he would forget his umbrella.

3. The future of the past (*futur du passé*) indicates an action that follows a time in the past. It is formed the same way as the present conditional.

Il m'a dit qu'il *partirait* à sept heures.	He told me he would leave at seven o'clock.

Present Time

When the indicative present is used in the main clause, the choice of tense used in the dependent clause depends upon the time of its action in relation to the present — whether it is simultaneous to, precedes, or follows the action in the main clause. Or, as in the last two examples, the tense of the dependent clause may depend upon the time of another action.

Je *pense* qu'elle *part* **maintenant.**	I think she is leaving now.
Elle *dit* qu'elle *partira* à dix heures.	She says that she's going to leave at ten o'clock.
Il *dit* qu'elle *est partie* à sept heures.	He says that she left at seven o'clock.
Tu *sais* qu'elle *cherchait* une situation.	You know that she was looking for a job.
Nous *savons* qu'elle *avait* déjà *accepté* cette offre.	We know that she had already accepted this offer.

Past Time
Imparfait vs Passé Composé (or passé simple)

In order to understand when to use either the *imparfait* or the *passé composé* (or the *passé simple*), imagine that you are seeing a movie and that you want to describe its story line. When the frames, or actions, follow each other quickly on the screen, in a series of short scenes — separate actions which are over and done quickly — they should be described in either the *passé composé* or the *passé simple*. But when the cameraman lingers on a scene — a long scene with not much happening — the scene should be described in the *imparfait*.

Long scene:

Le soleil *se couchait* à l'horizon et le cavalier solitaire *s'éloignait* à toute allure dans sa direction.	The sun was setting on the horizon and the lone horseman was moving toward it at full speed.

Short, quick scenes:

Un groupe d'Indiens *est apparu* (or *apparut*) sur le haut de la colline.	A group of Indians appeared at the top of the hill.
Ils *ont regardé* (or *regardèrent*) le soleil couchant et *ont vu* (or *virent*) le cavalier.	They looked toward the sunset and saw the horseman.

Other Past Tenses

The tense used in the dependent clause is always one tense removed (back or ahead) from the past tense used in the main clause, unless the actions are simultaneous.

Je *savais* qu'elle *cherchait* une situation.	I knew she was looking for a job.
Je ne *savais* pas qu'elle *avait* *déjà accepté* cette offre.	I didn't know she had already accepted that offer.
Elle *a dit* qu'elle *partirait* à dix heures.	She said she would leave at ten o'clock.
Je ne *savais* pas qu'elle *était partie* à sept heures.	I did not know she had gone at seven o'clock.

Special Uses of the Imperfect

1. The imperfect (*imparfait*) must be used after a main clause using *dire, croire, demander, se demander, estimer,* or *penser* in the past.

Il *a pensé* qu'elle *voulait* l'embrasser.	He thought that she wanted to kiss him.

2. The imperfect functions as a present-in-the-past in dependent clauses starting with a relative pronoun (when the main clause is in the past).

J'*ai vu* un homme qui *portait* un chapeau.	I saw a man who was wearing a hat.
Nous *avons acheté* le piano dont je te *parlais*.	We bought the piano I told you about.

3. The imperfect also functions as a present-in-the-past in dependent clauses expressing time, cause or consequence.

Elle *déjeunait* au moment où vous *avez téléphoné*.	She was having lunch when you phoned.

Future Time

Here again, as with main clauses in the present, the choice of tense in the dependent clause depends upon the time of its action in relation to the future-time action of the main clause.

Elle *partira* quand elle *sera* prête.	She will leave when she is ready.
Donne mon cadeau à ta grand-mère quand tu *arriveras*.	Give my present to your grandmother when you arrive.
J'*irai* la voir puisque tu me l'*as demandé*.	I will go see her since you asked me.
Elle *sera rentrée* à midi.	She will be back at noon.

NOTE: In French the future is used after *quand, lorsque, dès que,* and *aussitôt que* when future time is implied.

Conditional Sentences

Note the sequence of actions in the following table and the corresponding examples given below.

Dependent Clause	Main Clause
1. *Si* plus the present indicative	(a) Present Indicative
	(b) Future
	(c) Future Perfect
	(d) Imperative
2. *Si* plus the passé composé	(a) Present Indicative
	(b) Future
	(c) Future Perfect
	(d) Imperfect
	(e) Passé Composé
	(f) Imperative
3. *Si* plus imperfect	(a) Conditional
	(b) Past Conditional
4. *Si* plus pluperfect	(a) Conditional
	(b) Past Conditional

1. Si je *sors* maintenant, j'*emmène* le chien.

   If I go out now, I am taking the dog.

   Si tu *sors* ce soir, tu *emmèneras* le chien.

   If you go out tonight, you'll take the dog.

   Si elle *sort* maintenant, elle *sera* rentrée dans une heure.

   If she goes out now, she'll be back in an hour.

   Si vous *sortez*, emmenez le chien.

   If you go out, take the dog.

2. Si tu *as* bien *appris* tes leçons, tu ne *peux* pas les oublier.

   If you learned your lessons well, you can't forget them.

   Si nous *avons fait* nos devoirs, nous *aurons* une bonne note.

   If we have done our homework, we'll get a good grade.

   Si vous *avez* déjà *fait* cette tâche, vous *aurez fini* rapidement.

   If you have already done this task, you'll be finished quickly.

   S'il ne t'*a* pas *saluée*, c'est qu'il *était* distrait.

   If he did not greet you, it is because he was absent-minded

   S'il ne vous *a* pas *appelé*, c'est qu'il n'*a* pas *reçu* votre lettre.

   If he has not called you, it must be that he has not received your letter.

   Si nous ne *sommes* pas *rentrés* à dix heures, appelez la police.

   If we have not come back by ten o'clock, call the police.

3. Si tu *voyais* Venise, tu ne l'*oublierais* jamais.

   If you saw Venice, you'd never forget it.

   Si tu *payais* tes dettes regulièrement, tu ne *serais* jamais *endettée*.

   If you paid your debts regularly, you would never be in debt.

4. Si elles nous *avaient écrit*, nous *aurions* des nouvelles de la famille.

   If they had written us, we would have news from the family.

   Si vous *aviez eu* du courage, vous n'*auriez* pas *refusé*.

   If you had had the courage, you would not have refused.

Sentences Calling for the Subjunctive

In a dependent clause where the verb is in the subjunctive, the tense of the verb depends: (1) on the tense of the verb in the main clause and (2) on the relationship of the dependent clause with the main clause. In the following table, the tenses in italics are those used exclusively in literature.

Main Clause	Dependent Clause
1. Indicative Present or Future	Subjunctive Present or Past
2. Passé Composé	Subjunctive Present or Past
3. *Passé Simple,* Imperfect, or Pluperfect	Subjunctive *Imperfect* or *Pluperfect*
4. Present Conditional	Subjunctive Present or Past
5. Past Conditional	Subjunctive Present or Past; Subjunctive *Imperfect* or *Pluperfect*

1. Nous *sommes* contents qu'il *fasse* beau.

   We are happy that the weather is nice

   Nous *serons* contents que tu *fasses* ce voyage.

   We will be happy that you go on that trip.

   Je *suis* heureux que vous *ayez pu* faire ce voyage.

   I am glad that you could take this trip.

   Il *ira* dans les Alpes à moins qu'il n'*ait neigé.*

   He will go to the Alps unless it has snowed.

2. Il *a fallu* qu'il *vienne* au mauvais moment!

   He had to come at a bad time!

   Elle *a regretté* que ça se *soit passé* comme ça.

   She was sorry that it had happened that way.

3. Ils *passèrent* le col sans difficultés bien qu'il *neigeât.*

   They went through the pass even though it was snowing.

   Il *fallait* qu'il *fît* ce voyage en janvier.

   He had to take that trip in January.

   On *était parti* sans qu'elles nous *eussent entendus.*

   We had gone without their having heard us.

4. Je *voudrais* que vous *fassiez* la vaisselle.

   I would like you to do the dishes.

   Il *faudrait* que nous *soyons arrivés* à Naples la semaine prochaine.

   It is necessary that we arrive in Naples next week.

5. Il *aurait fallu* que vous *fassiez* réparer la voiture avant de partir.

   It would have been necessary for you to have the car repaired before leaving.

   Aurait-il *été* possible qu'ils *aient acheté* la maison à ce moment-là?

   Would it have been possible for them to buy the house at that time?

   Nous *aurions préféré* qu'il n'*eût* rien *dit.*

   We would have preferred for him to have said nothing.

   Est-ce que tu *aurais préféré* qu'ils *fussent* plus riches?

   Would you have preferred for them to have been richer?

11. Auxiliary Verbs

In addition to the auxiliary verbs *avoir* and *être,* which are used in the perfect tenses, there are other verbs that have a similar function before an infinitive. They may be auxiliary of time, of mode, or of aspect.

Aller + Infinitive

To express the immediate future (*le futur proche*) of the present, future, or past time (imperfect), one uses the verb *aller* followed by an infinitive. This construction is equivalent to "to be going to."

Je *vais* **lui** *répondre* **tout de suite.**	I am going to answer him right away.
Tu *allais* **lui** *répondre* **hier, mais tu ne l'as pas fait.**	You were going to answer him yesterday, but you did not do it.
Tu n'*iras* **pas m'***accuser* **de négligence!**	You are not going to accuse me of negligence!

Venir de + Infinitive

To express the immediate past (*le passé immédiat*) of present, future, or past time (imperfect), one uses *venir de* before an infinitive. This is the equivalent of "to have just."

Ton père *vient de rentrer.*	Your father just came home.
Nous *venions d'arriver* **quand vous avez téléphoné.**	We had just arrived when you phoned.

Être en train de

To emphasize the duration of an action, one may use *être en train de* + infinitive. This expresses the idea of doing something or of being in the process of doing something.

Je *suis en train de travailler.*	I am working.
Elle *était en train de faire des confitures.*	She was making jam.

Devoir

Devoir has many meanings, depending on the tense in which it is used.

Ça *devrait* **être bon.**	It ought to be good.
Votre maison *doit* **être belle.**	Your house must be beautiful.
Je *dois* **être au bureau à neuf heures et demie.**	I have to be at the office at nine-thirty.

Être sur le point de

This verb expresses the sense of "to be about to," "to be on the verge of."

Il *était sur le point de* **partir.**	He was about to leave.

Être loin de

This verb is used to express the sense of being far from doing something or being far from being something.

Marc *est* **bien** *loin d'être* **bête.**	Marc is far from being stupid.

Ce n'est pas pour

This verb is always used in the negative.

Ce n'est pas pour **me déplaire.**	This is not displeasing to me.

Faillir

This verb is used to express the meaning of nearly doing something or for something to nearly happen.

Il *a* **bien** *failli mourir.*	He nearly died.

Laisser

This verb means to let someone do something or to let something happen.

Laissez-**le** *partir.*	Let him go.
Il faut *laisser faire* **les choses.**	One must let things go their way.

Paraître and Sembler

Le ciel *paraît changer* **de couleurs.**	The sky seems to change colors.
Il *semble comprendre.*	He seems to understand.

Pouvoir and Vouloir

Il *voulait partir* **mais ne** *pouvait* **pas** *se lever.*	He wanted to leave but could not get up.

12. The Present Participle

The present participle (*le participe présent*) is formed by replacing the *-ons* ending of the first person plural present of regular verbs with the ending *-ant*. The present participle can be used as a verbal form, an adjective, or as part of a clause.

Infinitive	Present Participle
aimer	aimant
finir	finissant
vendre	vendant

A few present participles are irregular: *sachant (savoir), étant (être), ayant (avoir)*. See Chapter 8, Irregular Verbs, for other irregular present participles.

1. The present participle is used as a verbal form to express an action simultaneous with the action of the main verb. It is invariable when used in this way.

C'est une jolie bague, *valant* plus de mille dollars.	It's a pretty ring, worth more than a thousand dollars.
Une secrétaire *parlant* plusieurs langues vaut son pesant d'or.	A secretary speaking several languages is worth her weight in gold.
Connaissant le problème, il hésita.	Knowing the problem, he hesitated.

2. Adjectives formed with present participles agree in gender and number with the nouns they modify.

Ils ont *l'eau courante* dans leur ferme.	They have running water in their farm.
C'est *une rue passante*.	It's a busy street.
Nous allons samedi à *une soirée dansante*.	We're going to a dancing party next Saturday.

3. The gerund is formed with a present participle and the preposition *en*. The gerund modifies a verbal clause to express (a) the manner, (b) the means, (c) the cause, or (d) the time at which the action of the main clause took place. The two actions are simultaneous.

(a) Il faisait la grimace *en mangeant* ses escargots.	He was making a face while eating his snails.
Elle est arrivée *en sifflotant*.	She arrived whistling lightly.
(b) Les enfants sont arrivés *en courant*.	The children came running.
En faisant un grand effort, il a réussi à sauter par-dessus la barrière.	Making a tremendous effort, he was able to jump over the fence.

(c) C'est *en forgeant* qu'on devient forgeron.

It is by forging that one becomes a blacksmith.

Il est arrivé à se faire une belle situation *en travaillant* dur.

He managed to get a nice job by working hard.

(d) *En attendant,* elle est bien malheureuse.

In the meantime, she is very unhappy.

En passant devant elle, il admira sa robe.

When he passed in front of her, he admired her dress.

13. Active and Passive Voices

In the active voice, the subject performs an action. In the passive voice, the subject receives the action or is acted upon.

Active:	**Le feu a détruit notre sapin de Noël.**	Fire destroyed our Christmas tree.
Passive:	**Notre sapin de Noël a été détruit par le feu.**	Our Christmas tree was destroyed by fire.

The passive construction is formed with any tense of the verb *être* and a past participle. The past participle always agrees in number and gender with the subject. It is followed by *par* if the action is physical and *de* if it is mental.

Tout le monde aimait Jean. (*active*)	Everybody liked Jean.
Jean est aimé de tout le monde. (*passive*)	Jean is liked by everyone.
Une vague a renversé notre bateau. (*active*)	A wave tipped over our boat.
Notre bateau a été renversé par une vague. (*passive*)	Our boat was tipped over by a wave.

NOTE: *On* is never used in the passive voice. Pronominal (reflexive) verbs cannot be used in the passive voice.

Conjugation of the Passive Voice

Simple Tenses		Perfect Tenses	
Present	je suis aimé(e)	Past Perfect	j'ai été aimé(e)
Imperfect	j'étais aimé(e)	Pluperfect	j'avais été aimé(e)
Future	je serai aimé(e)	Future Perfect	j'aurai été aimé(e)
Passé Simple	je fus aimé(e)	Preterite Perfect	j'eus été aimé(e)
Present Subjunctive	je sois aimé(e)	Past Subjunctive	j'eusse été aimé(e)
Present Conditional	je serais aimé(e)	Past Conditional	j'aurais été aimé(e)
Infinitive	être aimé(e)	Past Infinitive	avoir été aimé(e)
Present Participle	étant aimé(e)	Past Present Participle	ayant été aimé(e)

14. Verbs Followed by a Preposition

1. The following verbs require the preposition *à* when followed by an infinitive. The preposition is not always translated into English.

aider (quelqu'un) à	to help (someone) to	**encourager (quelqu'un) à**	to encourage (some-one) to
s'amuser à	to amuse oneself (by)	**forcer (quelqu'un)**	to force (someone) to
apprendre à	to learn (how) to	**s'habituer à**	to get used to
avoir à	to have to	**s'intéresser à**	to be interested in
avoir de la peine à	to have difficulty (in)	**inviter (quelqu'un) à**	to invite (someone) to
commencer à	to begin (to)	**réussir à**	to succeed (in)
continuer à	to continue (to)		

Il est tellement malade qu'il *a de la peine à se lever*.   He is so sick that he has difficulty getting up.

2. The following verbs require the preposition *de* when followed by an infinitive.

s'arrêter de	to stop	**avoir de la chance de**	to be lucky to
cesser de	to stop	**avoir envie de**	to want to
choisir de	to choose to	**avoir hâte de**	to be in a hurry to
décider de	to decide to	**avoir le droit de**	to have the right to
se dépêcher de	to hurry	**avoir le temps de**	to have the time to
essayer de	to try to	**avoir peur de**	to be afraid of
finir de	to finish	**avoir raison de**	to be right to
oublier de	to forget to	**avoir tort de**	to be wrong to
refuser de	to refuse to	**en avoir assez de**	to have enough of

3. Some verbs can be followed by both *à* (followed by a person) and *de* (followed by the infinitive).

conseiller à (quelqu'un) de (faire quelque chose)	to advise (someone) to do something	**offrir à...de**	to offer (to someone) to
		permettre à...de	to allow (someone) to
défendre à...de	to forbid (someone) to	**promettre à...de**	to promise (someone) to
demander à...de	to ask (someone) to	**proposer à...de**	to propose (to someone) to
dire à...de	to tell (someone) to	**suggérer à...de**	to suggest (to someone) to

J'ai conseillé à ma fille de partir en vacances.   I advised my daughter to go on vacation.

Paul *a dit à sa sœur de se taire*.   Paul told his sister to shut up.

4. Some verbs can be followed directly by an infinitive.

aimer to love (to)	**espérer** to hope to
aimer bien to like (to)	**falloir** to be necessary
aimer mieux to prefer	**pouvoir** can, to be able to
aller to be going to	**préférer** to prefer
compter to intend to	**regarder** to look at
désirer to wish to	**savoir** to know how to
détester to detest	**souhaiter** to wish
devoir to have to, to be obligated to	**voir** to see
écouter to listen	**vouloir** to want, to wish
entendre to hear	

J'aimerais mieux partir **plus tard.**   I'd rather leave later.
Nous *savons faire* **du vélo.**   We know how to ride a bike.
Je *l'ai entendu tomber.*   I heard him fall.

5. The verb *compter* sometimes takes the prepositions *sur* and *pour*.

compter sur (quelqu'un) pour faire (quelque chose)

Je *compte sur* **toi** *pour* **préparer**   I am counting on you to prepare
   les hors d'œuvre.   the hors d'œuvre.

Part Two:
Essentials of Grammar

15. Articles

	Singular	Plural	
Definite Article: *the*	le	les	*(m.)*
	la	les	*(f.)*
	l'	les	*(m. & f.)*
Indefinite Article: *a, an, some*	un	des	*(m.)*
	une	des	*(f.)*

The Definite Article

The definite article, *le, la, les,* agrees in number and gender with the noun. *L'* replaces *le* or *la* before a noun starting with a vowel or a mute *h.*

Singular		Plural	
le livre	the book	les livres	the books
la carte	the map	les cartes	the maps

l'eau *(f.)*	the water
l'air *(m.)*	the air
l'étudiant *(m.)*	the student (male)
l'étudiante *(f.)*	the student (female)

Contractions:

The preposition *à* contracts with *le* and *les.* It does not contract with *la* or *l'.*

$$à + le = au$$
$$à + les = aux$$

Je parle *au* facteur.	I am speaking to the mailman.
Il parle *aux* étudiants.	He is speaking to the students.
Nous allons *à* l'université.	We go to the university.
Ils rentrent *à la* maison.	They are going home.

The preposition *de* also contracts with *le* and *les.* It does not contract with *la* or *l'.*

$$de + le = du$$
$$de + les = des$$

Elle parle *du* professeur.	She is talking about the teacher.
Nous parlons *des* étudiantes.	We are talking about the students.
Elles parlent *de la* voisine.	They are talking about the neighbor.
Ils parlent *de* l'économie.	They are talking about the economy.

Uses

The definite article is used with:

1. Nouns used in a general or abstract sense and collective nouns.

L'or **est précieux.**	Gold is precious.
Les enfants **sont en vacances.**	The children are on vacation.
La gourmandise **est un péché.**	Gluttony is a sin.
Les gens **sont malheureux.**	People are unhappy.

2. Adjectives and verbs used as nouns.

Elle préfère *le vert.*	She prefers green.
Le manger **et** *le boire.*	Food and drinks.

3. Names of languages.

Il ne parle que *l'anglais.*	He speaks only English.
Le français **est sa langue maternelle.**	French is his native tongue.

NOTE: The definite article is not used after the verb *parler*, after *en*, or after *de* (in an adjective phrase).

Ici, on parle *français.*	French is spoken here.
Combien de livres avez-vous lus en *français?*	How many books have you read in French?
J'ai perdu mon livre *de latin.*	I have lost my Latin book.

4. Titles of rank or profession.

le docteur **Freud**	Doctor Freud
le général **de Gaulle**	General de Gaulle
le président **de la République**	the President of the Republic

NOTE: The definite article is omitted in numerical titles of monarchs.

François Premier	François the First
Henri IV	Henry the Fourth

5. Geographical names.

La Corse **fait partie de** *la France.*	Corsica is part of France.
Le Rhône **se jette dans** *la mer Méditerranée.*	The Rhône river flows into the Mediterranean Sea.
Il va *au Canada.*	He is going to Canada.

NOTE: Names of cities, towns, and villages do not take an article, except those which are qualified by an adjective or a clause, and those that already have an article in their name *(La Nouvelle Orléans, Le Havre)*.

J'adore *Paris.*	I love Paris.
Le vieux Québec.	Old Quebec.
Le Lyon que je connais.	The Lyon I know.

NOTE: The names of some islands do not take the article: *Madagascar, Tahiti, Haïti, Hawaï.*

6. Names of seasons.

Je déteste *l'hiver*. I hate winter.
Nous reviendrons *au printemps*. We will come back in the spring.

7. Units of measure.

Ces pommes coûtent cinq francs *la livre*. These apples cost 5 F. a pound.
On achète ce matériel *au mètre*. You buy this material by the meter.

8. Dates.

Nous sommes *le vingt-cinq décembre*. It's the 25th of December.
Paris, *le 14 juillet 1983*. Paris, July 14, 1983.

The Indefinite Article

The indefinite article, *un, une, des,* agrees in number and gender with the noun.

Singular	Plural
un livre a book	**des livres** (some) books
une carte a map	**des cartes** (some) maps
J'ai *un ami* à Paris.	I have a friend in Paris.
Tu vas prendre *des pommes frites*?	Are you going to have french fries?

In the negative, *un, une,* and *des* are replaced by *de.*

Tu as *une carte*? Do you have a map?
Non, je *n'ai pas de* carte. No, I don't have a map.

NOTE: For further information on the negative, see Chapter 24.

Omission of the Article

The definite and indefinite articles are omitted in the following circumstances:

1. After the exclamatory adjective *quel (quelle, quels, quelles).*

Quelle foule! What a crowd!

2. Before the numbers *cent* and *mille.*

Tu me l'as répété *cent* fois. You told me a hundred times.
J'ai *mille et une* choses à faire. I have a thousand and one things to do.

3. In enumerations, if the nouns are understood to be all in the same category.

Ils ont invité *les parents, amis et connaissances* des jeunes mariés. They have invited the parents, friends, and acquaintances of the newlyweds.

4. Before days, months, time of day, and some holidays.

Lundi prochain, **je vais chez** **le médecin.**	Next Monday, I am going to the doctor.
Mai **est un joli mois.**	May is a pretty month.
Midi **sonne.**	It's striking noon.
Noël **au balcon,** *Pâques* **aux tisons.**	Christmas on the balcony, Easter around a fire. (*old French saying*)

NOTE: When expressing a repeated action, the definite article is used with days of the week.

Le dimanche, **nous mangeons de la** **pâtisserie au dessert.**	Every Sunday, we eat pastry for dessert.

NOTE: The article is used with *La Toussaint* (November 1st), *la Pentecôte* (Pentecost), and *le Mardi gras.*

5. In addresses.

Elle habite le boulevard **Saint-Germain.**	She lives on Saint-Germain Boulevard.

The Partitive

The partitive, *du (m.), de la (f.), de l' (m. & f.),* and *des (plural),* meaning "some," is used before nouns that cannot be counted or that indicate an undetermined quantity.

Je mange *du pain, du beurre* **et de** *la confiture* **au petit déjeuner.**	I eat bread, butter, and jam for breakfast.
Donne-moi *des fruits.*	Give me some fruit.
Il a bu *de l'eau* **toute la journée.**	He drank water all day.

The negative is expressed with *de* ("any").

Veux-tu *du pâté?*	Do you want pâté?
Merci, je *ne* **veux** *pas* *de pâté.*	No, thank you, I don't want any pâté.

16. Nouns

Gender

All nouns in French are either masculine or feminine. For nouns denoting things, the gender is purely coincidental. For people and animals, the gender is determined by the sex. The two nouns may then be entirely different or belong to the same family.

People

le fils son	la fille daughter
le garçon boy	la fille girl
l'homme (*m.*) man	la femme woman
le héros hero	l'héroïne (*f.*) heroine
le dieu god	la déesse goddess
l'oncle (*m.*) uncle	la tante aunt

Animals

le cheval horse	la jument mare
le coq rooster	la poule hen
le singe monkey	la guenon monkey
le taureau bull	la vache cow

1. Some nouns have the same form in both masculine and feminine.

l'artiste (*m.*)	l'artiste (*f.*)	artist
le camarade	la camarade	friend, comrade
le touriste	la touriste	tourist

2. In many cases, the feminine form of a noun is formed by adding an -*e* to the masculine form.

le cousin	la cousine	cousin
l'ami (*m.*)	l'amie (*f.*)	friend
l'étudiant (*m.*)	l'étudiante (*f.*)	student

3. Some masculine nouns ending in -*n* or -*t* double the consonant before adding an -*e* to form the feminine.

le lion	la lionne	lion, lioness
le paysan	la paysanne	peasant
le chat	la chatte	cat
le cadet	la cadette	the youngest

4. The feminine form of a noun ending in *-er* is formed with *-ère*.

le boulanger	la boulangère	baker
l'étranger (*m.*)	l'étrangère (*f.*)	stranger, foreigner
l'ouvrier (*m.*)	l'ouvrière (*f.*)	worker
le couturier	la couturière	fashion designer

5. The feminine form of a noun ending in *-eur* can be formed with *-euse*.

le coiffeur	la coiffeuse	hairdresser
le danseur	la danseuse	dancer
le menteur	la menteuse	liar

Some masculine nouns ending in *-teur* end in *-trice* in the feminine.

le directeur	la directrice	director
l'inspecteur	l'inspectrice	inspector
le manipulateur	la manipulatrice	manipulator

A few nouns in *-eur* do not have feminine forms, even when describing a female.

le chauffeur   driver
le professeur   teacher, professor
le docteur   doctor

NOTE: There is, however, now a trend to say *la prof.*

6. Some feminine nouns are formed by adding *-sse* to the masculine form.

le maître	master	la maîtresse	mistress
l'âne (*m.*)	donkey	l'anesse (*f.*)	donkey
le comte	count	la comtesse	countess
l'hôte (*m.*)	host	l'hôtesse (*f.*)	hostess
le prince	prince	la princesse	princess

7. A few nouns, whether referring to male or female, are always feminine.

une relation   an acquaintance
la personne   person
la victime   victim

8. A few nouns, whether referring to male or female, are always masculine.

l'auteur (*m.*)	author	le peintre	painter
le diplomate	diplomat	le poète	poet
l'écrivain (*m.*)	writer	le soldat	soldier
le juge	judge	le témoin	witness

9. A noun ending in *-f* changes to *-ve* in the feminine form.

le juif	la juive	Jew
le veuf	la veuve	widower, widow

10. Most nouns ending in *-x* change to *-se* in the feminine.

l'époux(*m.*)	l'épouse (*f.*)	spouse
l'orgueilleux (*m.*)	l'orgueilleuse (*f.*)	proud one

Plural of Nouns

The plural of nouns is usually formed by adding -*s* to the singular form. This is true of both masculine and feminine nouns.

la maison	house	les maisons	houses
le patron	boss	les patrons	bosses
la patronne	boss	les patronnes	bosses

1. Nouns ending in -*s*, -*x*, or -*z* do not change in the plural.

le pois	pea	les pois	peas
la croix	cross	les croix	crosses
le fils	son	les fils	sons
le nez	nose	les nez	noses

2. Nouns ending in -*al* change to -*aux* in the plural.

le canal	canal	les canaux	canals
le journal	newspaper	les journaux	newspapers
l'hôpital (*m.*)	hospital	les hôpitaux	hospitals

NOTE: *Le bal, le carnaval, le festival* take an -*s* (*les bals, les carnavals, les festivals*).

3. Nouns ending in -*au*, -*eau*, or -*eu* take an -*x* in the plural.

le noyau	pit (of a fruit)	les noyaux	pits
le manteau	coat	les manteaux	coats
le jeu	game	les jeux	games

4. Nouns ending in -*ou* take an -*s* in the plural, with the exception of these seven nouns:

le bijou	les bijoux	jewel(s)
le caillou	les cailloux	pebble(s)
le chou	les choux	cabbage(s)
le genou	les genoux	knee(s)
le hibou	les hiboux	owl(s)
le joujou	les joujoux	little toy(s)
le pou	les poux	louse (lice)

5. A few nouns have totally irregular plurals.

le ciel	sky	les cieux	heavens
l'œil	eye	les yeux	eyes

6. Nouns ending in -*ail* form the plural with -*s* except for a few.

le travail	work	les travaux	works
le vitrail	stained glass window	les vitraux	stained glass windows

7. Some nouns are usually used in the plural.

les ciseaux (*m.*)	scissors	les gens (*m.*)	people
les environs (*m.*)	surroundings	les lunettes (*f.*)	eyeglasses
les fiançailles (*f.*)	engagement	les mathématiques (*f.*)	mathematics
les frais (*m.*)	expenses	les mœurs (*f.*)	mores, customs
les funérailles (*f.*)	funeral	les vacances (*f.*)	vacation

NOTE: *Le ciseau* ("chisel"), *la lunette* (a kind of telescope), and *la vacance* ("vacancy") carry different meanings in the singular.

8. Some nouns are composed of two words. These nouns form their plurals like other nouns.

un pourboire	des pourboires	tips
un passeport	des passeports	passports
un portefeuille	des portefeuilles	wallets

Others form their plurals with the two words.

monsieur sir	messieurs sirs	
madame lady	mesdames ladies	
mademoiselle miss	mesdemoiselles misses (young ladies)	
un bonhomme chap	des bonshommes chaps	
un gentilhomme gentleman	des gentilshommes gentlemen	

9. The various rules (and their exceptions) for the plural formation of compound nouns are so complex, even for a French speaker, that only a few general statements will be made here.

Some compound nouns composed of adjectives and nouns pluralize both parts of the compound.

le beau-frère	les beaux-frères	brothers-in-law
le chou-fleur	les choux-fleurs	cauliflowers
le cerf-volant	les cerfs-volants	kites
le rouge-gorge	les rouges-gorges	robins
le coffre-fort	les coffres-forts	safes

NOTE: The adjective *grand* does not change in the feminine plural of compound nouns.

les grand-mères	grandmothers
les grand-tantes	great-aunts

Some compound nouns composed of verbs and nouns do not change in the plural.

le casse-cou	les casse-cou	daredevils
le gratte-ciel	les gratte-ciel	skyscrapers
le rendez-vous	les rendez-vous	appointments
le coupe-papier	les coupe-papier	letter openers
le pare-brise	les pare-brise	windshields

Some compounds composed of verbs and nouns pluralize the noun only.

le couvre-lit	les couvre-lits	bedspreads
le passe-montagne	les passe-montagnes	ski masks
le pique-nique	les pique-niques	picnics

The following compound nouns take an -*s* in the singular; they do not change in the plural.

le casse-noisettes   nutcracker
le cure-dents   toothpick
le chasse-mouches   flyswatter
le porte-avions   aircraft carrier
le porte-bagages   luggage rack
le porte-parapluies   umbrella stand
le presse-papiers   paperweight

Compound nouns that contain a preposition are often invariable.

le, les pied-à-terre   temporary lodging
le, les tête-à-tête   private conversations
le, les hors-d'œuvre   appetizers

But:

le chef-d'œuvre, les chefs-d'œuvre   masterpieces
l'arc-en-ciel, les arcs-en-ciel (*m.*)   rainbows

In a compound noun that contains an invariable word, that word always remains invariable.

| **l'après-midi** (*m.*) | **les après-midi** | afternoons |

An adjective that is part of a compound noun is pluralized.

| le nouveau-venu | les nouveaux-venus | newcomers |
| le dernier-né | les derniers-nés | last born children |

But:

| le nouveau-né | | les nouveau-nés the newly born |

10. In general, words borrowed from other languages take an -*s* in the plural.

l'agenda (*m.*)	les agendas	le club	les clubs
l'album (*m.*)	les albums	le forum	les forums
l'alibi (*m.*)	les alibis	la jeep	les jeeps
l'auditorium (*m.*)	les auditoriums		

But the following can also be found:

| un maximum | des maxima | un erratum | des errata |

NOTE: For the sake of accuracy, it is best to consult a dictionary to check the current usage in the plural formation of a specific compound noun.

17. Adjectives and Adverbs

Adjectives

Agreement of Adjectives

An adjective (or a past participle used as an adjective) agrees in gender and number with the noun or the pronoun it modifies, whether as a direct modifier or as a predicate adjective. An adjective modifying nouns of different genders is in the masculine plural.

le cahier *vert*	the green notebook
la robe *verte*	the green dress
les cahiers *verts*	the green notebooks
les robes *vertes*	the green dresses
Le cahier est *vert.*	The notebook is green.
La robe est *verte.*	The dress is green.
Le cahier et la robe sont *verts.*	The notebook and the dress are green.

NOTE: Adjectives of color follow the noun. When two adjectives of color are used, one qualifying the other, they are both invariable.

les yeux *bleu clair*	light blue eyes
des robes *vert foncé*	dark green dresses

Gender of Adjectives

The feminine of an adjective is usually formed by adding -*e* to the masculine form.

Le panier est *rond.*	The basket is round.
La table est *ronde.*	The table is round.
Il est *grand.*	It is big.
Elle est *grande.*	It is big.

1. An adjective that ends in -*e* in the masculine singular does not change in the feminine.

le cahier *rouge,* la jupe *rouge*	the red notebook, the red skirt
le garçon *belge,* la femme *belge*	the Belgian boy, the Belgian woman

2. Adjectives that end in -*el,* -*eil,* or -*nul* in the masculine singular double the -*l* before adding -*e* to form the feminine. This is also true of *gentil.*

gentil	gentille	nice
nul	nulle	not one
cruel	cruelle	cruel
vermeil	vermeille	vermilion, bright red

3. Some adjectives have alternate masculine singular forms that are used before a word beginning with a vowel or a mute *h*.

masc. sing.	alt. masc. sing.	fem. sing.	masc. plur.	fem. plur.	
beau	bel	belle	beaux	belles	beautiful
fou	fol	folle	fous	folles	crazy
mou	mol	molle	mous	molles	soft
nouveau	nouvel	nouvelle	nouveaux	nouvelles	new
vieux	vieil	vieille	vieux	vieilles	old

4. Adjectives that end in *-en* and *-on* double the *n* before adding *-e* to form the feminine.

algérien, algérienne Algerian
ancien, ancienne ancient, former
bon, bonne good
breton, bretonne from Brittany
moyen, moyenne average

5. Most adjectives ending in *-et* or *-l* double the *t* or *l* before adding *-e* to form the feminine.

muet, muette silent, mute
net, nette clean, spotless
quel, quelle which, what
tel, telle such

NOTE: *Complet* ("complete"), *incomplet* ("incomplete"), *concret* ("concrete"), *discret* ("discreet"), *indiscret* ("indiscreet"), *inquiet* ("worried"), and *secret* ("secret") take the ending *-ète: complet, complète*.

6. Most adjectives that end in *-s* in the masculine singular take an *-e* in the feminine form.

gris, grise gray

But the following adjectives double the *s* before adding *-e*.

bas, basse low   **gras, grasse** fat
épais, épaisse thick   **gros, grosse** big, stout

NOTE: *Frais* becomes *fraîche*.

7. An adjective ending in *-x* in the masculine singular changes to *-se*.

heureux, heureuse happy
jaloux, jalouse jealous

NOTE: *Faux* ("false") and *roux* ("reddish-brown") become *fausse* and *rousse*.

8. A few adjectives whose masculine forms end in *-f* change to *-ve* in the feminine.

actif, active active   **neuf, neuve** new
bref, brève brief   **vif, vive** alive, lively
captif, captive captive

9. Some adjectives whose masculine forms end in -*c* change the -*c* to -*que* in the feminine.

public, publique public

NOTE: *Blanc* ("white") and *franc* ("frank") become *blanche* and *franche; sec* ("dry") becomes *sèche*.

10. Adjectives ending in -*g* in the masculine singular change to -*gue*.

long, longue long
oblong, oblongue oblong

11. Adjectives ending in -*gu* add -*ë*.

aigu, aiguë sharp
ambigu, ambiguë ambiguous

12. Most adjectives ending in -*eur* have the feminine forms -*euse* or -*trice*.

menteur, menteuse lying   **producteur, productrice** productiv
trompeur, trompeuse deceptive, misleading   **protecteur, protectrice** protective
voleur, voleuse thieving

NOTE: *Antérieur, postérieur, ultérieur, extérieur, intérieur, majeur, mineur, supérieur, inférieur,* and *meilleur* form the feminine with -*e*.

13. A small number of adjectives are irregular.

favori, favorite favorite
malin, maligne shrewd, cunning
rigolo, rigolote funny

Number

The plural of most adjectives is formed by adding -*s* to the singular (masculine or feminine) form. All feminine adjectives have regular plurals. Only masculine adjectives are irregular.

1. Masculine adjectives ending in -*s* or -*x* do not change in the plural.

un manteau gris   **des manteaux gris**   gray coats
un vent doux   **des vents doux**   soft winds

2. A masculine adjective ending in -*eau* takes -*x* in the plural.

un beau chapeau   **de beaux chapeaux**   beautiful hats
un nouveau parapluie   **de nouveaux parapluies**   new umbrellas

NOTE: A plural noun preceded by a plural adjective takes *de* instead of *des*.

3. Adjectives ending in -*al* generally change to -*aux*.

un soldat loyal   **des soldats loyaux**   loyal soldiers

NOTE: But *naval* ("naval"), *fatal* ("fatal"), *natal* ("native"), and *final* ("final") take -*s*.

4. *Tout* ("all") has the plural *tous*.

Position of Adjectives

1. In general, a descriptive adjective follows the noun it modifies.

un lion féroce	a ferocious lion	**une pièce immense**	a huge room
un homme sérieux	a serious man		

2. Some descriptive adjectives precede the noun.

une belle maison	a beautiful house	**un vieux chat**	an old cat
une bonne journée	a good day	**un joli arbre**	a pretty tree
un vilain tableau	an ugly painting	**une nouvelle maison**	a new house

3. Certain descriptive adjectives are placed before or after the noun, depending on their meaning.

une maison ancienne	an old house	**un grand homme**	a great man
une ancienne amie	a former friend	**un homme grand**	a tall man
une chambre propre	a clean room	**un homme brave**	a brave man
ma propre chambre	my own room	**un brave homme**	a fine
la semaine dernière	last week (the week before)		(good) man
		une histoire vraie	a true story
la dernière semaine	the last week (of a series)	**une vraie bête**	a real beast
		un vieillard pauvre	a poor (needy) man
une voiture chère	an expensive car		
un cher cousin	a dear cousin	**un pauvre vieillard**	a poor (to be pitied) man
une personne seule	a person alone		
une seule personne	only one person		

4. Indefinite adjectives usually come before the noun.

plusieurs	several	**autre**	other
chaque	every, each	**même**	same
quelque	some, a few	**tel, telle**	such
tout(e)	all	**certain**	certain

quelques object rares	a few rare objects
plusieurs choses	several things
toutes les mères	all the mothers

A few indefinite adjectives change meaning depending on their position.

l'idée même	the very idea	**une certaine réussite**	a certain amount of success
la même idée	the same idea	**une réussite certaine**	an unqualified success

Comparison of Adjectives

1. To form a comparative of inequality, place *plus* ("more") or *moins* ("less") before the adjective and *que* after the adjective. A comparative of equality is formed by placing *aussi* ("as") before the adjective and *que* after the adjective.

Inequality:

Marc est *plus grand que* **Catherine.**   Marc is taller than Catherine.
Catherine est *moins grande que* **Marc.**   Catherine is less tall than Marc.

Equality:

Marc est *aussi intelligent que* **Catherine.**   Marc is as intelligent as Catherine.
Catherine n'est pas *aussi sportive que* **Marc.**   Catherine is not as sportive as Marc.

2. To form the superlative, place the definite article before the comparative and *de* after the adjective.

C'est *le plus grand de* **tous.**   He is the tallest of them all.
Marc est *le plus grand* **élève** *de*   Marc is the tallest student in
  sa classe.   his class.

Irregular Comparison

Comparatives			Superlatives	
bon	**meilleur**	better	**le (la) meilleur(e)**	the best
mauvais	**pire**	worse	**le (la) pire**	the worst
petit	**moindre**	less (in importance)	**le (la) moindre**	the least

NOTE: In some cases, *plus mauvais* and *le plus mauvais* are used instead of *pire* and *le pire*. *Plus petit* and *le plus petit* are used to compare size.

Adverbs

Adverbs are invariable words that modify verbs.

Adverbs of Manner

1. Most adverbs of manner are formed by adding the suffix *-ment* to the feminine singular form of the adjective.

grave	**grave**	**gravement**	seriously
long	**longue**	**longuement**	for a long time, at length
complet	**complète**	**complètement**	completely
vif	**vive**	**vivement**	vivaciously

2. A few adjectives change the mute *-e* to *-é* before the suffix.

énorme	**énormément**	enormously
profonde	**profondément**	deeply

3. Usually, when the masculine form of the adjective ends with a vowel, *-ment* is added to the masculine form.

joli	**jolie**	**joliment**	prettily
vrai	**vraie**	**vraiment**	really

NOTE: *Gai (gaie),* however, becomes *gaiement* ("gaily").

4. Masculine singular adjectives ending in -*ant* and -*ent* form adverbs ending in -*amment* and -*emment* (which replace the -*nt* ending of the adjective).

suffisant	**suffisamment**	sufficiently
prudent	**prudemment**	prudently

NOTE: One common exception to this rule is *lent.*

lent	**lente**	**lentement**	slowly

5. Some common adverbs of manner not ending in -*ment* include:

ainsi	like this, thus	**plutôt**	rather
bien	well	**tard**	late
debout	up, standing	**tôt**	early
comme	how	**vite**	quickly
exprès	on purpose	**volontiers**	gladly
mal	badly	**ensemble**	together

Position of Adverbs of Manner

1. Adverbs modifying verbs in a simple tense are usually placed after the verb.

Je vous l'envoie directement.	I am sending it to you directly.

2. In perfect tenses, the position of adverbs varies: As a guideline, place adverbs of more than one syllable after the verb, and those of one syllable between the auxiliary and the past participle.

Je vous l'ai envoyé directement.	I sent it to you directly.

3. Short adverbs come before an infinitive.

Apprenez à bien conduire!	Learn to drive well!

4. Adverbs of manner are placed before the adjective or adverb they modify.

Elle est bien habillée.	She is well dressed.
Il parlait plutôt mal.	He spoke rather badly.

Comparison of Adverbs

Regular comparison of adverbs is like that of adjectives, with *plus, aussi,* and *moins* placed before the adverb and *que* after.

Inequality:

Je mange *moins mal* **ici** **qu'au restaurant.**	I eat less badly here than in a restaurant.
Nous voyageons *plus régulièrement* **que** **l'année dernière.**	We are traveling more regularly than last year.

Equality:

Elle parle *aussi fort que* **son père.**	She speaks as loudly as her father.

Superlative:

Le plus souvent, il dort après le repas.	Most often, he sleeps after meals.

Irregular Comparisons

Adverb	Comparative	Superlative
bien well	mieux better	le mieux the best
mal badly	pis, plus mal worse	le pis, le plus mal the worst
beaucoup much	plus more	le plus the most
peu little	moins less	le moins the least

NOTE: When a clause introduced by *que* follows an affirmative comparison of inequality, *ne* is used before the verb in the dependent clause.

Marie est *plus sportive que* je ne le croyais.	Marie is more sportive than I thought.

Adverbs of Quantity

1. Adverbs of quantity are used with a verb, before a comparative, before a noun with *de,* and before the adverbs *plus, moins,* and *trop.*

assez enough	davantage more
autant as much	plus more
beaucoup much, a lot	moins less
combien how much	très very
ne...guère hardly	trop too much
peu little	ne...pas du not at all tout
presque almost	la plupart most

Il est *beaucoup* plus bavard que moi.	He is much more talkative than I.
Je n'ai pas *assez* d'argent.	I don't have enough money.

2, *Bien des* is used in the sense of *beaucoup de.* It is followed by a noun.

Bien des voyages se terminent mal.	Many trips end badly.

3. *Aussi* is used before an adjective or an adverb.

Vous avez couru *aussi* vite que moi.	You ran as fast as I did.

NOTE: If the sentence is negative, *si* is used instead of *aussi.*

(adjective)

Elle n'est pas *si* timide que vous croyez.	She is not as timid as you think.

(adverb)

Il ne travaille pas *si* vite qu'il en a l'air.	He doesn't work as fast as he seems to.

18. Possession

Possession with *De*

A phrase with the preposition *de* ("of") followed by a person's name or a noun is used to indicate possession.

la voiture de Philippe	Philippe's car
la queue du chat	the cat's tail
la fleur du pommier	the apple tree's bloom

Possessive Adjectives

Possessive adjectives are placed before the noun and agree in number and gender with the thing possessed, not the possessor.

Masculine Singular	Feminine Singular	Masculine and Feminine Plural
mon, ton, son	ma, ta, sa	mes, tes, ses
my, your, his (her)	my, your, his (her)	my, your, his (her)
	notre, votre, leur	nos, vos, leurs
	our, your, their	our, your, their

mon crayon	my pencil	ses parents	his (her) parents
ton stylo	your pen	notre maison	our house
son frère	his (her) brother	votre appartement	your apartment
ma table	my table	leur mère	their mother
ta chaise	your chair	nos voitures	our cars
sa sœur	his (her) sister	vos télévisions	your televisions
mes cahiers	my notebooks	leurs parents	their parents
tes livres	your books		

NOTE: Before a noun beginning with a vowel or a mute *h*, the masculine forms *mon, ton,* and *son* are used instead of *ma, ta,* and *sa*.

mon aventure (*f.*)	my adventure
ton horloge (*f.*)	your clock
son équipe (*f.*)	his (her) team

The definite article is used instead of the possessive adjective when speaking of parts of the body. Note that the past participles in the following example sentences are invariable.

Il lui a tendu *les* bras.	He opened his arms to her.
Je vais me laver *les* mains.	I am going to wash my hands.
Elle s'est cassé *la* jambe.	She broke her leg.

Possessive Pronouns

The possessive pronouns are always preceded by a definite article and agree in gender and number with the thing possessed.

le mien, la mienne	mine	les miens, les miennes	mine
le tien, la tienne	yours	les tiens, les tiennes	yours
le sien, la sienne	his (hers)	les siens, les siennes	his (hers)
le nôtre, la nôtre	ours	les nôtres	ours
le vôtre, la vôtre	yours	les vôtres	yours
le leur, la leur	theirs	les leurs	theirs

Ma cravate est moche. Donne-moi *la tienne!*	My necktie is ugly. Give me yours!
Voilà *la mienne.*	Here is mine.
Mes parents vont bien. Et *les vôtres?*	My parents are well. And yours?

1. The definite articles *le* and *les* preceding possessive adjectives contract with *à* and *de*.

Ne parlons pas de mon travail. **Parlons** *du vôtre.*	Let's not talk about my work. Let's talk about yours.
A votre santé! A *la* **bonne** *vôtre!*	To your health! To yours!
J'ai écrit à mes parents. Mon cousin n'a pas écrit *aux siens.*	I have written my parents. My cousin has not written his.

2. To express possession with the verb *être,* one can also use the emphatic pronouns *moi, toi, lui, elle, nous, vous, eux,* and *elles.*

Ce stylo est *à toi?* **Non, il est** *à eux.*	This pen belongs to you? No, it's theirs.

3. Some idiomatic expressions with possessive adjectives and pronouns:

Il l'a fait *de son propre chef.*	He did it on his own initiative.
Dites-lui bien des choses *de ma part.*	Give him my best.
Elle était *des nôtres* **pour Noël.**	She was with us at Christmas time.

19. Demonstrative Adjectives and Pronouns

Demonstrative Adjectives

Singular	Plural
ce, cet *(m.)* } cette *(f.)* } this, that	ces these, those

The demonstrative adjective precedes and agrees in number and gender with the noun it modifies. The masculine form *cet* is used before a noun beginning with a vowel or a mute *h*.

ce matin	this (that) morning
cet été	this (that) summer
cette plage	this (that) beach
ces maillots de bain	these (those) swimming suits

1. When it is necessary to make a distinction between "this" and "that," or "these" and "those," -*ci* and -*là* may be added to the noun, -*ci* referring to things close to the speaker, *là* to things further away.

Ce plat-*ci* est meilleur que ce plat-*là*.	This dish is better than that dish.

2. Demonstrative adjectives must be repeated before each noun.

ce livre et cette lampe	this book and this lamp
ces garçons et ces filles	these boys and girls

However, when a noun is preceded by several descriptive adjectives applying to the noun, the demonstrative adjective is not repeated.

ce bel et bon seigneur	this beautiful and good lord

Demonstrative Pronouns

Singular	Plural
celui *(m.)* } this, this one, celle *(f.)* } that, that one	ceux *(m.)* } these, those celles *(f.)* }

As-tu pris ton écharpe? Non, j'ai pris *celle* de Claudette.	Did you take your scarf? No, I took Claudette's.
Quel autobus vas-tu prendre? *Celui* qui passe boulevard Saint-Michel.	What bus are you going to take? The one that goes on Saint-Michel Boulevard.

1. A demonstrative pronoun always refers to someone or something mentioned previously. It is often followed by -*ci* or -*là* to convey the meaning of "this one" or "that one."

Quelle glace préfères-tu?	Which ice cream do you prefer?
Celle-ci ou *celle-là?*	This one or that one?

2. The demonstrative pronouns may be followed by the relative pronouns *qui, que,* or *dont.*

C'est *celui-là qui* **te plaît?**	Is it that one you like?
Celle *que* **je t'ai donnée est plus jolie.**	The one I gave you is prettier.
Ce sont *ceux dont* **je t'ai parlé.**	They are the ones I spoke to you about.

3. A demonstrative pronoun may be followed by *de* to indicate possession.

Voilà mon parapluie et voilà *celui de* **ma sœur.**	Here is my umbrella and here is the one that belongs to my sister (my sister's).

4. *Ceci* and *cela* are invariable pronouns that refer to facts, ideas, or things not named specifically.

Tout *ceci* **me chagrine.**	All this pains me.
Tout *cela* **m'est égal.**	I don't care about all that.

5. *Ce* may be used as an invariable demonstrative pronoun and translated as "it," "he," "she," "this," "that," "they," "these," "those."

Ce is used as subject of the verb *être* when the verb is followed by a modified noun, a proper noun, a pronoun, or a superlative.

Modified noun:

C'est un grand homme.	He is a great man.
Ce fut une fête mémorable.	It was a memorable party.

NOTE: The personal pronouns *il, ils, elle,* and *elles* are used when *être* is followed by an adjective or a noun by itself.

Il est grand.	He is tall.
Elle est médecin.	She is a physician.

Proper noun:

C'est Claude qui a écrit.	It was Claude who wrote.
Qui est-ce? C'est Simone.	Who is it? It's Simone.

Demonstrative and possessive pronoun:

C'est celui-là que j'aime.	It's that one I like.
C'est le vôtre?	Is it yours?

Superlative and *seul:*

C'est le plus grand homme que j'aie rencontré.	That's the tallest man I have ever met.
Est-ce le seul que vous ayez?	Is it the only one you have?

NOTE: *Ce* before *être* often repeats a subject already expressed.

Mon meilleur ami, c'est vous.	My best friend is you.
Les plats que je préfère, ce sont les plats préparés en sauce.	The dishes I prefer are those prepared with a sauce.
Partir, c'est mourir un peu.	To leave is to die a little.

Ce is used with *être* when the verb is followed by an adjective modified by an infinitive. The infinitive, then, is preceded by the preposition *à*.

Ce n'est pas facile à faire.	It's not easy to do.
C'était difficile à deviner.	It was difficult to guess.

Ce can be used when the verb *être* is preceded by the verbs *devoir, pouvoir,* or *aller*.

Ce doit être une plaisanterie.	It must be a joke.
Ce peut être une erreur.	It could be a mistake.

NOTE: The impersonal pronoun *il* is used when *être* is followed by an adjective, itself modified by an infinitive, to represent a concept or an idea. In this case, the infinitive is preceded by *de*. If the concept applies to another person, *que* is used, followed by the subjunctive.

Il est préférable de partir tout de suite.	It is preferable to leave right away.
Il est préférable que tu partes tout de suite.	It is preferable that you leave right away.

6. *Ça,* a reduced form of *cela,* is invariable and is used commonly in various expressions.

Ça y est.	That's it.
À part ça	Aside from that
Ça suffit.	That's enough.
Ça a l'air d'une soucoupe volante!	It looks like a flying saucer.
Ça va? Ça va mal.	How are things? Things are not going well.
Ne faites pas ça!	Don't do that!
C'est comme ça.	That's the way it is.
Comme ci comme ça.	So-so.
C'est pour ça.	That's why.
Comment ça se fait?	How come?
Ça ne fait rien!	It doesn't matter!

20. Personal Pronouns

Subject Pronouns

A subject pronoun is the subject of a verb. The speaker is called the first person; the one spoken to is the second person; and the one spoken of is the third person.

	Singular	Plural
1st person	je (j') I	nous we
2nd person	tu you	vous you
3rd person	il, elle, on he, she, one (we, etc.)	ils, elles they

1. *On* is a convenient indefinite pronoun used only as a subject. Commonly used in everyday conversation, it can have the meaning of "we," "someone," "one," "people," "everyone." In writing, it can also mean "I," "he," "she," "you," "they." When *on* is used with *être* and an adjective, the adjective takes the number and gender of the person or persons represented by *on*.

On va au cinéma?	Shall we go to the movies?
On était petites à cette époque-là.	We (girls) were little at the time.

2. In French there are two pronouns used to express "you": *tu* and *vous*. The familiar *tu* is used to address relatives, friends, classmates, children, and animals. *Vous* is used when speaking to an adult, a stranger, or more than one person.

Marc, as-tu fini de taquiner ton frère?	Marc, will you stop teasing your brother?
Bonjour, Madame Ogier. Comment allez-vous?	Good morning, Mrs. Ogier How are you?
Bonjour, mes enfants. Comment allez-vous?	Good morning, children. How are you?

3. *Il* and *elle* stand for persons ("he," "she") as well as for animals and inanimate objects ("it"). The gender of the pronoun is the same as the gender of the noun it replaces.

Jean se promène avec son chien. *Il* en est très fier.	Jean is taking a walk with his dog. He is very proud of him.
J'aime *la vitesse,* mais *elle* tue.	I like speed, but it kills.
Ma chatte est gourmande. *Elle* mange toute la journée.	My cat is a glutton. She eats all day long.

Emphatic Pronouns

Corresponding to the subject pronouns, the emphatic pronouns are:

moi	nous
toi	vous
lui	eux
elle	elles
soi	

1. The emphatic pronouns are used to emphasize the subject or the object pronoun.

J'habite à Paris. Et *toi?*	I live in Paris. And you?
Où est-ce que tu l'as connu, *lui?*	Where did you meet *him?*

2. An emphatic pronoun is used after a preposition.

Voulez-vous vous promener *avec moi?*	Do you want to go for a walk with me?
Mettez-vous *derrière lui.*	Go behind him.

3. The emphatic pronouns are used after verbs that take the prepositions *à* and *de* and after verbs of motion.

Je penserai *à toi.*	I'll think of you.
Laissez venir *à moi* **les petits enfants.**	Let the little children come to me.
Il se méfie *de toi.*	He is suspicious of you.

4. An emphatic pronoun may be part of a sentence without a verb.

Qui a mangé le gâteau? *Pas moi.*	Who ate the cake? Not I.

5. An emphatic pronoun can be used with *ce* and *être*.

Qui est le plus bête? *C'est lui.*	Who is the stupidest? It's him.
Ce sont eux **qui le disent.**	It's they who say so.

6. In comparisons, or with *ni. . .ni* or *ne. . .que,* emphatic pronouns are used.

Michel est plus intelligent que *lui.*	Michel is smarter than he.
Je n'aime que *toi.*	I love only you.
Je n'inviterai *ni lui ni elle.*	I'll invite neither him nor her.

7. The emphatic pronouns are used after commands. When *en* is used, *moi* and *toi* become *m'* and *t'*.

Écoute-moi!	Listen to me!
Parlez-m'en!	Talk to me about it!

8. *Soi* is used after a preposition when the subject of the verb is *on, chacun,* or *personne*.

Chacun pour soi.	To each his own.
On n'a jamais confiance qu'en soi-même.	One only trusts oneself.

9. *Même* after an emphatic pronoun is used to emphasize even more that it is the person talked about who did the action, and conveys the idea of "self" in English.

Je préfère le faire *moi-même.*	I prefer to do it myself.
C'est *eux-mêmes* **qui me l'ont dit.**	They told me themselves.

Reflexive Pronouns

Reflexive pronouns are those used with pronominal verbs. (See Chapter 4.) They, too, correspond to the subject pronouns.

me	nous
te	vous
se	se

Se is also used with the infinitive: *s'habiller* ("to get dressed"), *se lever* ("to get up").

Nous nous amusons **à la ville.**	We enjoy ourselves in town.
Vous vous ennuyez **à la campagne.**	You are getting bored in the country.

Direct Object Pronouns

The direct object pronoun receives the action of the verb. It is placed before the verb.

me	me	nous	us
te	you	vous	you
le	him, it	les	them
la	her, it		

Si tu n'es pas gentil, je ne *t'*aimerai plus.	If you are not nice, I won't love you any more.
Ma vieille robe? Je *l'*ai **donnée aux pauvres.**	My old dress? I gave it to the poor.
Le jeune chien *la* **léchait gentiment.**	The young dog licked her gently.

Indirect Object Pronouns

The indirect object pronoun denotes the person to, for, or from whom something is given, told, sent, etc. It is placed before the verb.

me	to me	nous	to us
te	to you	vous	to you
lui	to him, to her	leur	to them

Maman va *leur* téléphoner.				Mom is going to phone them.
Je *lui* ai donné leur numéro de téléphone.				I gave her their telephone number.
Est-ce que je *te* l'ai donné aussi?				Did I give it to you also?

Table of Personal Pronouns

Subject	Direct Object	Indirect Object	Reflexive	Emphatic
je (j')	me (m')	me (m')	me (m')	moi
tu	te (t')	te (t')	te (t')	toi
il	le (l')	lui	se (s')	lui
elle	la (l')	lui	se (s')	elle
on			se (s')	soi
nous	nous	nous	nous	nous
vous	vous	vous	vous	vous
ils	les	leur	se (s')	eux
elles	les	leur	se (s')	elles

Y and *En*

As a pronoun, *y* refers to places, things, or ideas that have already been mentioned. *Y* often replaces *à* (or another preposition) + a place, thing, or idea.

Vas-tu à la banque? Oui, j'y vais.	Are you going to the bank? Yes, I'm going there.
Est-il derrière le garage? Non, il n'y est pas.	Is he behind the garage? No, he is not there.
Pensez-vous aller au théâtre? Oui, j'y pense.	Are you thinking of going to the theater? Yes, I'm thinking about it.

En refers to things, places, and ideas. It often replaces *de* + a noun.

Des lions? Il *en* a tué beaucoup.	Lions? He killed a lot of them.
Tu as des disques de jazz? Oui, j'*en* ai une douzaine.	Do you have jazz records? Yes, I have a dozen of them.
Vous sortez de l'école à 3 h? Oui, nous *en* sortons à 3 h.	Do you leave school at three o'clock? Yes, we leave (there) at three o'clock.

Double Object Pronouns

More than one object pronoun may be used in a sentence. In that case, the pronouns appear in a certain order before the verb.

me					
te	le (l')	lui			
se	la (l')		y	en	*verb*
		leur			
nous	les				
vous					

Je *le lui* ai dit hier.	I said it to him yesterday.
Nous *lui en* avons parlé hier.	We spoke to him about it yesterday.
Tu *les y* as vues?	Did you see them there?
Ne *m'en* parle pas!	Don't tell me about that!

Order After the Verb

Object pronouns are placed after the verb in an affirmative imperative sentence.

		moi		
		toi		
	le	lui		
verb	la	nous	y	en
	les	vous		
		leur		

Offre-*lui* des bonbons!	Give him candy! Give him a lot!
Offre-*lui-en* beaucoup!	
Vends-*les-leur!* Ils ne nous font jamais de cadeaux!	Sell them to them! They never give us any presents!
Apporte-*moi* la bouteille, mais ne la casse pas!	Bring me the bottle, but don't break it!

21. Relative Pronouns

A relative pronoun occurs in a dependent clause and describes or refers to a noun or a group of words in the main clause.

Simple Forms			Compound Forms			
			Singular		Plural	
			Masc.	Femi.	Masc.	Femi.
who, that, which	qui	which	lequel	laquelle	lesquels	lesquelles
whom, that, which	que	of which	duquel	de laquelle	desquels	desquelles
of whom, of which	dont	to which	auquel	à laquelle	auxquels	auxquelles

Simple Forms

1. *Qui* is used as the subject of the verb, *que* as the object. *Dont* replaces *de* + a form of *lequel*.

C'est une de mes cousines *qui* m'a invitée à la campagne.	It's one of my cousins who invited me to the country.
C'est le bateau *que* je voulais acheter.	It's the boat I wanted to buy.
As-tu entendu le concert *qu'*on a donné hier à la télé?	Did you hear the concert that was on TV yesterday?
Voilà le journal *dont* je vous ai parlé.	Here is the newspaper I talked to you about.

2. *Où* can be used as a relative pronoun to refer to an antecedent of time or place.

C'est là *où* j'aimerais aller.	That's where I would like to go.
C'est l'année *où* j'ai gagné un prix.	It was the year I won a prize.

Compound Forms

1. The forms of *lequel* can be the object of a preposition and usually refer to things, although they may also be used for people.

C'est la raison *pour laquelle* on l'a renvoyé.	That's the reason for which he was fired.

2. *De* and *lequel* contract to become *duquel*. *Duquel* is often replaced by *dont*.

Le grand livre sur la table? *Duquel* parlez-vous?	The big book on the table? Which one are you talking about?

3. *Auquel* is a contraction of *à* + *lequel*. It is often replaced by *à qui* when referring to people.

C'est une chose *à laquelle* tu aurais dû penser.	That's something you should have thought about.
Le garçon *auquel (à qui)* tu parlais est portugais.	The boy you were talking to is Portuguese.

4. *Ce qui, ce que,* and *ce dont* are used when the antecedent is not precise, or is understood. *Ce qui* is the subject of the verb. *Ce que* is the object. *Ce dont* is used when the verb takes *de.*

Ce qui t'appartient m'appartient.	What belongs to you belongs to me.
Montre-moi *ce que* tu as trouvé.	Show me what you found.
Je ne suis pas d'accord avec *ce dont* tu parles.	I don't agree with what you are talking about.

NOTE: With *tout,* these forms express the idea of "all that" or "everything."

Tout ce qui brille n'est pas d'or.	All that glitters is not gold.
Je te donnerai *tout ce que* tu voudras.	I'll give you everything you want.

22. Interrogatives and Exclamations

Interrogatives

Interrogatives are classified as pronouns, adjectives, and adverbs.

Pronouns

	Persons	Things	Persons and Things
Subject of the Question	qui who qui est-ce qui who	qu'est-ce qui what	lequel laquelle which, which one lesquels lesquelles
Direct Object	qui whom qui est-ce que whom	que what qu'est-ce que what	lequel laquelle which, which one lesquels lesquelles
Object of a Preposition	qui whom	quoi what	lequel laquelle which, which one lesquels lesquelles

Qui m'attend?	Who is waiting for me?
Qui est-ce qui m'attend?	Who is waiting for me?
Qui attendez-vous?	Whom are you waiting for?
Qui est-ce que vous attendez?	Whom are you waiting for?
A qui avez-vous écrit?	To whom did you write?
Qu'est-ce qui vous ennuie?	What is bothering you?
Que vais-je faire?	What am I going to do?
Qu'est-ce qu'elle dit?	What is she saying?
A quoi pensez-vous?	What are you thinking about?
Lequel d'entre vous a fait ça?	Which one of you did that?
Laquelle allons-nous acheter?	Which one are we going to buy?
Desquels vous servirez-vous?	Which ones will you use?

1. When *qui, que,* and *quoi* are used as direct objects or are preceded by a preposition, there is inversion of the subject and verb.

Qui êtes-vous?	Who are you?
Que dis-je?	What am I saying?
Que puis-je faire pour vous?	What can I do for you?
Pour qui me prenez-vous?	Who do you think I am?

2. The forms *qui est-ce qui, qu'est-ce qui, qui est-ce que,* and *qu'est-ce que* do not call for inversion.

Qu'est-ce qui s'est passé?	What happened?
Qui est-ce qui te l'a dit?	Who told you so?

3. The forms of *lequel* always refer to someone or something that has to be chosen among others.

Voilà deux portes. Par laquelle entrerons-nous?	Here are two doors. Which one shall we go through?
Parmi tous ces vélos, lequel vas-tu acheter?	Among all these bikes, which one are you going to buy?
De tous vos amis étrangers, lesquels préférez-vous?	Of all your foreign friends, which ones do you prefer?

4. All three forms of *lequel* contract with *à* or *de.*

Un dentiste? Auquel vous adresserez-vous?	A dentist? Which one will you go to?
Vos cousines? Desquelles parlez-vous?	Your cousins? Which ones are you speaking of?

5. The pronoun *quoi* can sometimes be the subject of the question.

Quoi de plus facile?	What is easier?
Quoi d'autre?	What else?

6. *À qui* used with *être* shows ownership; *de qui* used with *être* expresses personal relationship or authorship.

A qui est ce tablier?	Whose apron is it?
De qui est ce livre?	Who is the author of this book?
De quoi êtes-vous fait?	What are you made of?

Adjectives

1. *Quel, quelle, quels, quelles* ("which," "what") are the forms of the interrogative adjectives. They agree in number and gender with the nouns they modify.

Quelles nouvelles m'apportez-vous?	What news did you bring me?
A quel hôtel descendrez-vous?	What hotel will you go to?

2. Used with the verb *être,* the interrogative adjective may be separated from the noun it modifies.

Quel est ce bruit?	What is that noise?

Adverbs

quand when	**d'où** from where
pendant combien de temps how long	**par où** from where
depuis combien de temps since when (length)	**pourquoi** why
depuis quand since when (date)	**comment** how
où where	**combien** how much, how many

Quand arrives-tu?	When are you coming?
Où irez-vous?	Where will you go?
Pourquoi partent-ils?	Why are they leaving?
Combien as-tu payé?	How much did you pay?

Exclamations

The forms of *quel* are used as exclamatory adjectives.

Quelle chance!	What luck!
Quel beau bateau!	What a beautiful boat!
Quels idiots!	What idiots!

Comme, combien, and *que* are also used in exclamations.

Comme il est beau!	How beautiful it is!
Vous ne pouvez pas savoir combien je l'aime!	You can't imagine how much I love her!
Que je suis content!	How glad I am!

23. Some Practical Rules

Question Formation

There are several ways to form questions in French. The sentence construction may be changed or the speaker's intonation may change.

1. One may form a question using the construction of a declarative sentence, but with rising intonation. This is very common in conversation.

Vous allez à l'église tous les dimanches?   You go to church every Sunday?

2. You may add *n'est-ce-pas?* to a declarative sentence, with rising intonation. This form is asking for confirmation.

Vous allez à l'église tous les dimanches, *n'est-ce-pas?*   You go to church every Sunday, don't you?

NOTE: *N'est-ce-pas?* is invariable.

3. *Est-ce que* may precede a declarative sentence (rising intonation). This formula is often used in conversation.

Est-ce que **vous allez à l'église tous les dimanches?**   Do you go to church every Sunday?

4. One may form an interrogative sentence using inversion. This formula is used more in writing than in conversation.

Allez-vous **à l'église tous les dimanches?**   Do you go to church every Sunday?

NOTE: The formula with *est-ce que* can be modified into *est-ce. . .qui, c'est . . .qui,* or *est-ce que c'est. . .qui.*

Est-ce **vous** *qui* **m'avez écrit?**   Is it you who wrote me?
C'est **lui** *qui* **a parlé le premier?**   Is it he who spoke first?
Est-ce que c'est **elle** *qui* **lui a répondu?**   Is it she who answered him?

Indirect Statements

An indirect statement may be reported in the present or the past. When reported in the present, the tense of the original (direct) statement does not change. When reported in the past, the tenses change according to the tense used in the original (direct) statement.

Present:	Pierre dit: "Je suis content."	Pierre dit qu'il est content.
	Pierre dit: "Je finirai mon travail ce soir."	Pierre dit qu'il finira son travail ce soir.
	Pierre dit: "J'ai fini mon travail."	Pierre dit qu'il a fini son travail.
Past:	Pierre a dit: "Je suis content."	Pierre a dit qu'il était content.
	Pierre a dit: "Je finirai mon travail ce soir."	Pierre a dit qu'il finirait son travail ce soir.
	Pierre a dit: "J'ai fini mon travail."	Pierre a dit qu'il avait fini son travail.

An interrogation is called indirect when the speaker is reporting a question asked by him or her or by a third party.

Direct: **Quand allez-vous arriver?**
Indirect: **Pierre m'a demandé quand on allait arriver.**

Direct: **Où est-ce que vous serez à huit heures?**
Indirect: **Pierre m'a demandé où nous serons à huit heures.**

Direct: **Prendrez-vous un taxi?**
Indirect: **Pierre m'a demandé si on prendrait un taxi.**

NOTE: There is no inversion in indirect questions.

24. Negatives

Non

Non is the adverb of negation most commonly used in French.

Apportez-vous de bonnes nouvelles?	Are you bringing good news?
Non.	No.
Veux-tu encore du dessert?	Do you want more dessert?
Non, j'en ai déjà repris.	No, I have already had seconds.

NOTE: After a negative statement or question, *si* is used instead of *oui*.

Tu n'as pas de voiture?	You don't have a car?
Mais *si*. **J'ai celle de Marc.**	Of course I do. I have Marc's.

Other Common Negatives

ne...pas	not	**ne...ni...ni**	neither...nor
ne...pas du tout	not at all	**ne...ni ne**	neither...nor
ne...point	not, not at all	**ne...que**	only
ne...plus	not any more, no more, no longer	**ne...aucun(e)**	no, none, no one
		ne...nul(le)	no, none, no one
ne...guère	hardly, scarcely	**ne...aucunement**	not at all, not in any way
ne...personne	no one, nobody		
ne...rien	nothing	**ne...nullement**	not at all, by no means

Qu'est-ce qu'il y a là-dedans?	What's in there? Nothing.
Il *n'y* **a** *rien*.	
Vous avez des frères et des sœurs?	Do you have brothers and sisters?
Non, je n'ai qu'un frère.	No, I only have one brother.

1. In simple tenses, *ne* precedes the verb, and *pas (plus, jamais,* etc.) follow the verb.

Je *ne* **veux** *pas* **ce livre.**	I don't want this book.
Il *ne* **vient** *jamais* **ici.**	He never comes here.

2. In perfect tenses, the second part of most negatives precedes the past participle.

Elle *n'est jamais* **montée à la Tour Eiffel.**	She never went to the top of the Eiffel Tower.

NOTE: *Personne, que,* and *aucun* follow the past participle.

Des lettres? *Non,* **il** *n'***a reçu** *aucune* **lettre.**	Letters? No, he received no letter.
Je *n'***ai invité** *personne* **pour ton anniversaire.**	I did not invite anyone for your birthday.

3. Both parts of a negative precede the infinitive.

Elle préfère *ne rien* **faire.**	She prefers to do nothing.
Il a fait semblant de *ne pas* **les voir.**	He pretended not to see them.

4. When the partitive is called for in a negative sentence, *pas de* replaces the partitive.

Tu as *du* **pain?** *Non,* **je** *n'***ai** *pas de* **pain.**	Do you have bread? No, I don't have bread.

5. *Ne. . .que* is the equivalent of "only" in French. *Que* comes before the word or words that are being restricted.

Ça *ne* **pouvait** *qu'***aggraver la situation.**	It could only have worsened the situation.

NOTE: When *seulement* ("only") is used to restrict the subject of a sentence, *ne* is omitted.

Seulement **lui aurait pu le faire.**	Only he could have done it.

6. *Rien, personne,* and *aucun* can also be used as subject pronouns. *Nul* is only used as a subject. In these cases, *ne* precedes the verb.

Rien ne **nous arrive jamais.**	Nothing ever happens to us.
*Personne n'***a parlé.**	No one spoke.
*Nul n'***est prophète en son pays.**	No one is a prophet in his own country.
Aucun **de ceux-là** *ne* **me plaît.**	None of these pleases me.

NOTE: The pronoun *personne* is masculine. The noun *personne* is feminine.

Personne ne **m'a parlé.**	No one spoke to me.
Il y avait deux *personnes* **qui étaient déjà arrivées.**	Two people had already arrived.

7. *Ni* precedes each word restricted by this negative.

Il *n'***y a** *ni* **sel** *ni* **poivre sur la table.**	There is neither salt nor pepper on the table.
Ils *n'***avaient** *ni* **faim** *ni* **soif.**	They were neither hungry nor thirsty.

8. In a few cases, *ne* is omitted. *Jamais* in this case takes the meaning of *ever.*

Plus **d'espoir!**	No more hope!
Auras-tu *jamais* **fini?**	Will you ever be finished?

NOTE: There are a few expressions or sayings in which *ne* is used without the second part of the negative.

*N'*importe!	No matter!
Si je *ne* me trompe. . .	If I am not mistaken. . .

NOTE: After *il y a, voilà*, or *voici* followed by a perfect tense, *ne* is often used alone.

Voilà longtemps que je *ne* t'ai vu.	It's been a long time since I saw you.

9. There are a few possible combinations of two or more negatives used with *ne*.

ne...plus guère	hardly ever	ne...jamais personne	never anyone
ne... plus personne	no one any more	ne...jamais rien	never anything
ne...plus rien	nothing any more	ne...jamais nulle part	nowhere any more
ne...plus jamais	never again	ne...jamais plus	never again

Je *ne* le vois *plus guère*.	I hardly ever see him.
Il *n'*y avait *plus personne*.	There was no one left any more.
Il *n'*y a *plus rien* à faire.	There is nothing left to do.
Tu *n'*invites *jamais personne*.	You never invite anyone.
Vous *ne* m'emmenez *jamais nulle part*.	You never take me anywhere.
Je *ne* le ferai *jamais plus*.	I will never do it again.
Je promets de *ne plus jamais* le faire.	I promise never to do it again.

10. *Ni. . .non plus* is used with nouns and emphatic pronouns.

Je n'en peux plus.	I can't go on any more.
Ni moi non plus.	Me neither.

Indefinite Pronouns

Indefinite pronouns, like indefinite adjectives (see page 70), refer either to something yet to be mentioned, or to something which has already been mentioned.

Tel est souvent pris qui croyait prendre.	He is often caught who thought he would be the one doing the catching.
Hélène et Jacqueline sont allées faire du ski. Pourtant, *l'une et l'autre* ont pris un train différent.	Helene and Jacqueline went skiing. Nevertheless, each took a different train.

Indefinite pronouns can be classed according to whether they are positive or negative in meaning.

Indefinite pronouns with a negative meaning

aucun(e) anyone, no one, nobody
nul no man, none
pas un(e) not one
personne nobody
rien nothing

NOTE: In sentences with these pronouns, *ne* must be used before the verb.

Rien *ne* **t'arrête.**   Nothing is stopping you.
Personne *ne* **s'est trompé.**   No one made a mistake.

Indefinite Pronouns with a positive meaning

These indefinite pronouns may refer to a unit, a group, or a whole.

> **on**   one, we, they, people, etc.
> **l'un(e)...l'autre**   the one...the other
> **un(e) autre**   another
> **n'importe qui**   anyone
> **n'importe quoi**   anything
> **quelqu'un, quelqu'autre**   someone, some other
> **quelque chose**   something
> **quiconque**   anyone
> **tel, un tel**   such (person, thing), such a
> **le même**   the same (person, thing)

As a group:

> **autrui**   others, other people
> **les uns...les autres**   the ones...the others
> **certains**   some (people, animals, things)
> **plusieurs**   several
> **plus d'un**   more than one
> **la plupart**   most of them
> **les mêmes**   the same ones

As a whole:

> **chacun(e)**   each one
> **tous**   everyone
> **tout**   all

NOTE: *On* may represent one or more persons. The corresponding possessive adjectives may be *son, sa,* or *ses.*

On **a** *ses* **habitudes.**   Each one of us has his own routine.
Ce n'est pas *n'importe qui.*   He is not just anyone.
—**A quoi penses-tu?** —A *quelque chose!*   —What are you thinking about? —Something!
Aucune **d'elles n'étaient jamais**   None of them had ever been
  allée en Inde.   to India.
Les uns **parlaient,** *les autres*   Some were speaking, the others
  écoutaient.   were listening.

NOTE: Indefinite adjectives were mentioned in the chapter dealing with adjectives (page 70). Many of them have the same form and meaning as the indefinite pronouns.

25. Prepositions

Like adverbs and conjunctions, prepositions are invariable. Prepositions are used to establish a rapport between two words or two groups of words in a sentence. They may precede nouns, verbs, adverbs, or phrases.

The Preposition À

1. The preposition *à* can follow a verb before an infinitive. (See the list of verbs that take *à* before an infinitive, Chapter 14.)

Chantal apprend *à* patiner.   Chantal is learning to skate.

2. *À* can be used to indicate place, time, or manner.

à droite to the right	**à pied** on foot
à loisir at leisure	**à mort** to death
à mon avis in my opinion	**à la main** handmade
à la campagne in the country	**à la maison** at home
à la française (in) the French way	**à ce moment-là** at that time

3. *À* can follow a verb before an indirect object.

Tu as donné cette viande *aux enfants*?   Did you give this meat to the children?
   Non, je l'ai donnée *au chien*.   No, I gave it to the dog.

4. *À* can also be used to indicate possession.

Cette voiture est *à toi*?   This car is yours?
   Non, elle est *à Christophe*.   No, it is Christophe's.

The Preposition *De*

1. *De* can come after a verb and before an infinitive. (See the list of verbs that take *de* before an infinitive, Chapter 14.)

Il s'arrête *de* courir.   He stops running.

NOTE: *De* is also used before an infinitive to become a predicate.

À vous *de* jouer!   Your turn to play!

2. *De* can be used to form an adverb.

de loin   from far away   **d'ici**   from here

3. *De* can also be used to form an adjective.

C'est tout ce qu'il y a *de plus* **vrai.**	It could not be more true.
Qu'est-ce que tu as fait *de beau?*	What did you do that was interesting?

4. *De* is also used to form a relation of time, point of view, cause, reason, or manner.

de l'heure	per hour	**d'instinct**	by instinct
de jour	by day	**de sang-froid**	in cold blood
de caractère	as for his (her) character	**de dépit**	in spite
		d'habitude	habitually

5. *De* may also be used to show possession. (See Chapter 18.)

C'est le tableau *de Nicole.*	That's Nicole's painting.

6. *De* also follows adverbs of quantity. (See Chapter 17.)

Julie a *beaucoup* **d'argent.**	Julie has a lot of money.

7. *De* comes after a noun that indicates quantity or measure or after a collective noun.

un litre *de* **lait**	a liter of milk
une paire *de* **bas**	a pair of stockings
une dizaine *de* **personnes**	about ten people
un million *de* **dollars**	one million dollars

NOTE: There is a difference in meaning between expressions using a noun + *à* and those using a noun + *de*.

un verre *de* **vin**	a glass of wine
un verre *à* **vin**	a wine glass
une tasse *de* **café**	a cup of coffee
une tasse *à* **café**	a coffee cup

8. *De* is used to express dimensions, to denote differences in age and measurement, and to denote English expressions of time.

La pièce a cinq mètres *de long.*	The room is five meters long.
Il est le plus âgé *de deux ans.*	He is older by two years.
Il est plus grand que Marc *de deux centimètres.*	He is two centimeters taller than Marc.
cinq heures *du matin*	5 A.M.
dix heures *du soir*	10 P.M.

9. *De* is also used in many adjective phrases.

un billet *de* **train**	a train ticket
un bureau *de* **tabac**	a tobacco store

10. *De* is used before the objects of some adjectives.

digne de foi	worthy of confidence
plein d'enthousiasme	full of enthusiasm
dur d'oreille	hard of hearing

À, *De,* and *En* with Place Names

To	à	cities	à Paris, à New York
	au, aux	countries (masculine), continents, provinces	au Portugal, aux États-Unis
	en	countries (feminine or beginning with a vowel or a mute *h*)	en Hollande, en Tunisie
From	de	cities, countries, continents, provinces (feminine or masculine beginning with a vowel or a mute *h*)	de Marseille, de Boston d'Allemagne
	de + *def. art.*	masculine countries, continents, provinces	du Québec, des Pays-Bas

Je vais *à* Beaune, *en* Bourgogne.	I am going to Beaune, in Burgundy.
Les Martin sont allés *au* Havre, *en* Normandie.	The Martins went to Le Havre, in Normandy.
Paul revient *du* Maroc. Il est allé *à* Marrakech.	Paul is coming back from Morocco. He went to Marrakesh.
Revenant d'un voyage *en* Italie et *au* Portugal, il est rentré fourbu *aux* États-Unis.	Coming back from a trip to Italy and Portugal, he came back exhausted to the States.

NOTE: When the place name is modified, *en* is replaced by *dans.*

Il va *en* Espagne.	He is going to Spain.
Il va *dans* l'Espagne de Don Quichotte.	He is going to the Spain of Don Quixote.

NOTE: When the idea of "inside" a city is conveyed, *dans* is used instead of *à.*

J'habite en plein *dans* Lyon.	I live in the center of Lyon.

NOTE: When place names are modified, *de* is replaced by *de la* or *du.*

Ils viennent *de la* belle province de Québec.	They come from the beautiful province of Quebec.
Nous aimons les quartiers *du* vieux Paris.	We love the districts of old Paris.

NOTE: Some cities contain an article in their names, which contract with *à* or *de.*

Mes parents reviennent *du* Caire. (Le Caire).	My parents are coming back from Cairo.

Other Uses of *En*

1. *En* can serve to form an adverb. (See Chapter 12.3, the formation of the gerund.)

Gérard entra *en* riant.	Gérard came in laughing.

2. *En* sometimes precedes a noun, a proper noun, an adjective, or a pronoun.

en soie	made of silk	en juin	in June
en laine	made of wool	en été	in summer
en noir	in black	en voiture	by car
en maths	in math	en marche	moving
en haut	upstairs	en bois	made of wood
en colère	angry	en fête	festive
en quoi	in what	en qui	in whom
croire en Dieu	to believe in God	de fil en aiguille	from thread to needle

3. *En* does not usually take an article after it, but both definite and indefinite articles are used in certain fixed expressions.

Il a dit ça *en l'air.*	He said that through his hat.
Nous buvons *en l'honneur de* tes vingt ans.	We are drinking in honor of your 20th birthday.
En ce temps-là, nous étions plus heureux.	At that time, we were happier.
J'aurai fini ça *en un mois.*	I'll have that finished in a month's time.

Other Prepositions

après after	depuis since, from	jusque up to, all the way to
d'après according to	dès at, as soon as	parmi among
auprès de· close to	devant in front of	sous under
avant before	pendant during	sur on, over
avec with	entre between	vers toward
contre against	envers toward	
dans in, inside	hors out of	

Nous habitons là *depuis* vingt ans.	We have lived there for twenty years.
Ils suivirent la route de Lyon, *depuis* Orléans *jusqu'à* Beaune.	They followed the road to Lyon, from Orléans to Beaune.
Ils se dirigent *vers* le jardin.	They are going toward the garden.
Soyez gentils *envers* votre frère.	Be nice to your brother.

1. *Par* may be used in the sense of "by" (agent or means), "through," "out of," "in," or "on."

On est parti *par* le train.	We left by train.
Regarde *par* la fenêtre!	Look out the window!
Ne sors pas *par* un temps pareil!	Don't go out in such weather!
Nous nous voyons deux fois *par* an.	We see each other twice a year.

2. *Pour* may mean "for," "in place of," "among," "in the interest of," etc.

Ce gâteau est *pour* mon filleul.	This cake is for my godson.
Je répondrai *pour* toi.	I'll answer for you.
Mourir *pour* son pays.	To die for one's country.
Je ne fais rien *pour* l'instant.	I am doing nothing for the moment.
Nous partons demain *pour* Berlin.	We are leaving tomorrow for Berlin.
Elle est grande *pour* une fille de son âge.	She is tall for a girl her age.

26. Conjunctions

Conjunctions, like prepositions and adverbs, are invariable. Conjunctions connect two clauses, words, or group of words that have the same function in a sentence. There are two classes of conjunctions: conjunctions of coordination and conjunctions of subordination.

Conjunctions of Coordination

1. Liaison

et	and	alors	well, then
ensuite	then	puis	then
comme	as	aussi	also, thus
ni	neither, nor		

2. Cause

car	since, because	en effet	indeed

3. Consequence

donc	thus	aussi	thus
alors	thus	ainsi	so
par conséquent	in consequence	c'est pourquoi	that's why
de toute façon	in any case		

4. Transition

or	now, then

5. Opposition

mais	but	et	and
au contraire	on the contrary	cependant	however
pourtant	yet	d'ailleurs	in any case

6. ou   or   soit...soit   either...or

7. c'est à dire   that is

Ensuite, ils sont tous allés au cinéma, *car* il faisait très mauvais. Mon père *et* ma mère, mon frère *ou* ma sœur, je ne me rappelle plus, *mais* pas moi. *Donc,* je suis resté tout seul à la maison. *De toute façon,* j'avais beaucoup de travail à faire. *Alors,* je ne me suis pas ennuyé.

Then they all went to the movies, because the weather was terrible. My father and my mother, my brother or my sister, I don't remember, but not I. Thus, I stayed home by myself. Anyway, I had a lot of work to do. Well then, I did not get bored.

Conjunctions of Subordination

The conjunctions of subordination serve to connect a dependent clause to the main clause.

1. Cause

comme   as
parce que   because

puisque   since
d'autant que   as far as

2. Consequence

que (+ *subj.*)   that
si bien que   so that

de sorte que   so that

3. Goal

afin que   in order that
tellement que   so much that

pour que   so that
de peur que   for fear that

4. Concession, opposition

bien que   though, although
quoique   although
alors que   when

quand même   just the same
malgré que   in spite of the fact that
sans que   without (gerund)

Janine s'est acheté un nouveau chapeau, *bien qu'***elle en ait des douzaines.**
Janine bought a new hat, even though she has dozens of them.

Il n'ose pas sortir *de peur que* **le vent ne le décoiffe.**
He does not dare go out, for fear that the wind will undo his hairdo.

Je veux pourtant qu'il sorte, *parce qu'***il ne prend jamais l'air.**
I want him to go out, however, because he never gets fresh air.

27. Time

Days of the Week

lundi Monday
mardi Tuesday
mercredi Wednesday
jeudi Thursday
vendredi Friday
samedi Saturday
dimanche Sunday

The days of the week are all masculine and are not capitalized. They are not usually preceded by a definite article, unless it is to express a repeated occurrence.

Aujourd'hui, c'est lundi.	Today is Monday.
Je travaille *le* samedi.	I work on Saturdays.
Mardi prochain, j'irai au cinéma.	Next Tuesday, I'll go to the movies.
À jeudi!	See you Thursday!

Months of the Year

janvier January
février February
mars March
avril April
mai May
juin June

juillet July
août August
septembre September
octobre October
novembre November
décembre December

The months of the year are masculine and are not capitalized.

Seasons of the Year

le printemps spring
l'été (*m.*) summer

l'automne (*m.*) fall, autumn
l'hiver (*m.*) winter

The Date

The ordinal *premier* is used for the first of each month. For all other dates the cardinal numbers are used.

Nous sommes le combien aujourd'hui?	
C'est le combien aujourd'hui?	What is the date?
Quelle date sommes-nous?	
C'est le premier mai.	It is the first of May.
C'est le deux mai. Le deux.	It's the second of May. The second.
Nous sommes le premier juin.	It's the first of June.
Nous sommes le vingt-trois juin.	It is the twenty-third of June.
Le vingt-trois.	The twenty-third.

The French write the date in the following manner: *le 5 avril 1983*

day / month / year
5 / 4 / 83 = le 5 avril 1983

Divisions of Time

la seconde	second	la nuit	night
la minute	minute	le jour, la journée	day
l'heure (*f.*)	hour	la semaine	week
la demi-heure	half an hour	le mois	month
le quart d'heure	a quarter of an hour	la saison	season
le matin, la matinée	morning	l'an (*m.*) l'année (*f.*)	year
l'après-midi (*f.*)	afternoon	le siècle	century
le soir, la soirée	evening		

NOTE: *Le matin, le soir, le jour,* and *l'an* are used when talking about a precise time; *la matinée, la soirée, la journée,* and *l'année* indicate a duration of time.

J'ai passé *un an* à Paris.	I spent a year in Paris.
Je n'ai rien fait de *toute l'année.*	I did nothing all year.
Passez dans *la matinée.*	Come sometime in the morning.

Expressions of Time

naintenant	now	demain matin	tomorrow morning
out de suite	right now	hier après-midi	yesterday afternoon
iujourd'hui	today	la semaine dernière	last week
:e matin	this morning	la semaine prochaine	next week
:e soir	tonight	toute la journée	all day
:et après-midi	this afternoon	tous les jours	every day
iier	yesterday	tout le temps	all the time
lemain	tomorrow	au début du mois	at the beginning of the month
ivant-hier	the day before yesterday	au milieu de la semaine	about the middle of the week
iprès-demain	the day after tomorrow	à la fin de l'année	at the end of the year
e matin	in the morning	quelque temps	sometime
'après-midi	in the afternoon	quelques jours	a few days
e soir	in the evening	à la mi-septembre	about mid-september
a nuit	at night	vers neuf heures	about nine o'clock

Time of Day

Quelle heure est-il?	What time is it?
Il est une heure.	It is one o'clock.
Il est deux heures.	It is two o'clock.
Il est midi.	It is noon.
Il est minuit.	It is midnight.
À quelle heure?	At what time?
À cinq heures (juste).	At five o'clock (sharp).
À six heures cinq.	At five past six.
À sept heures et quart.	At quarter past seven.
À huit heures et demie.	At eight-thirty.
À midi et demi.	At half past noon.
À dix heures moins le quart.	At quarter to ten.
À vingt-et-une heures quarante cinq.	At quarter to ten (P.M.) (9:45).
À onze heures moins dix.	At ten to eleven.
À vingt-deux heures cinquante.	At ten to eleven (P.M.) (10:50).

NOTE: The 24-hour clock is used in France for train, plane, bus, and theater schedules, and often for appointments.

22 heures = 10:00 P.M.

NOTE: *Demi* is masculine in the expressions *midi et demi* and *minuit et demi,* while *demie* agrees with *heure (f.)* in all other cases.

The Cardinal Points

le nord	north	le nord-est	northeast
le sud	south	le sud-est	southeast
l'est (*m.*)	east	le nord-ouest	northwest
l'ouest (*m.*)	west	le sud-ouest	southwest

28. Numbers and Units of Measurement

Cardinal Numbers

0 zéro	21 vingt et un	76 soixante-seize
1 un, une	22 vingt-deux	77 soixante-dix-sept
2 deux	23 vingt-trois	78 soixante-dix-huit
3 trois	24 vingt-quatre	79 soixante-dix-neuf
4 quatre	25 vingt-cinq	80 quatre-vingts
5 cinq	26 vingt-six	81 quatre-vingt-un
6 six	27 vingt-sept	90 quatre-vingt-dix
7 sept	28 vingt-huit	91 quatre-vingt-onze
8 huit	29 vingt-neuf	100 cent
9 neuf	30 trente	101 cent un
10 dix	31 trente et un	200 deux cents
11 onze	32 trente-deux	300 trois cents
12 douze	40 quarante	400 quatre cents
13 treize	50 cinquante	500 cinq cents
14 quatorze	60 soixante	600 six cents
15 quinze	70 soixante-dix	700 sept cents
16 seize	71 soixante et onze	800 huit cents
17 dix-sept	72 soixante-douze	900 neuf cents
18 dix-huit	73 soixante-treize	1000 mille
19 dix-neuf	74 soixante-quatorze	2000 deux mille
20 vingt	75 soixante-quinze	1.000.000 un million (de)
		1.000.000.000 un milliard

The plural -s is required after *cent* in even hundreds like *deux cents,* but is dropped when *cent* is followed by another number.

265   **deux cent soixante-cinq**

Above a thousand, numbers and dates can be read in thousands or in hundreds. *Mille* is often shortened to *mil.*

1983   **mil neuf cent quatre-vingt-trois**
          dix-neuf cent quatre-vingt-trois

Note also that a period or a blank is used in figures 1.000 and above; a comma is used to mark the division between whole numbers and decimals.

10 245   10.245   27,50

Other remarks: *Un* is used when counting and with masculine nouns; *une* is used with feminine nouns.

Odd and even numbers:

impair odd	**de deux en deux** by two's
pair even	**de dix en dix** by ten's

Les numéros impairs sont 3, 5, 7, etc.	The odd numbers are 3, 5, 7, etc.
Les numéros pairs sont 2, 4, 6, etc.	The even numbers are 2, 4, 6, etc.
Comptez de cinq en cinq, de cinq à cinquante.	Count by five's from five to fifty.

Collective Numbers

la paire (de) two, a pair of	**la centaine (de)** hundred
la dizaine (de) ten, about ten	**le millier (de)** thousand
la douzaine (de) a dozen	**le million (de)** million
la quinzaine (de) fifteen, about fifteen	**le milliard (de)** billion
la vingtaine (de) twenty	

Ordinal Numbers

1st	**premier, première**	17th	**dix-septième**
2nd	**deuxième, second(e)**	18th	**dix-huitième**
3rd	**troisième**	19th	**dix-neuvième**
4th	**quatrième**	20th	**vingtième**
5th	**cinquième**	21st	**vingt et unième**
6th	**sixième**	22nd	**vingt-deuxième**
7th	**septième**	30th	**trentième**
8th	**huitième**	40th	**quarantième**
9th	**neuvième**	50th	**cinquantième**
10th	**dixième**	60th	**soixantième**
11th	**onzième**	70th	**soixante-dixième**
12th	**douzième**	80th	**quatre-vingtième**
13th	**treizième**	90th	**quatre-vingt-dixième**
14th	**quatorzième**	100th	**centième**
15th	**quinzième**	1000th	**millième**
16th	**seizième**	1,000,000th	**millionième**

Ordinals may be abbreviated by using a figure and adding *-ème*. 1st adds *-er* or *-ère*, depending on the gender of the noun to which it refers. Ordinals precede the noun.

22ème	**le vingt-deuxième étage**	the twenty-third floor
1ère	**la première page**	the first page

Fractions

1/2 **demi(e)** (*adj.*)	1/6 **un sixième**	1/12 **un douzième**
la moitié (*noun*)	1/7 **un septième**	1/13 **un treizième**
1/3 **un tiers**	1/8 **un huitième**	1/14 **un quatorzième**
1/4 **un quart**	1/9 **un neuvième**	1/20 **un vingtième**
3/4 **trois-quart**	1/10 **un dixième**	1/100 **un centième**
1/5 **un cinquième**	1/11 **un onzième**	1/1000 **un millième**
	% **pour cent**	

Demi ("half") is an adjective and agrees in gender with the noun to which it refers.

une heure et demie   one o'clock

Demi is invariable when followed by a hyphen.

une demi-livre de sucre   half pound of sugar

La moitié ("half") is a noun.

J'ai mangé la moitié de la pomme.   I have eaten half of the apple.
La moitié de 4 est 2.   Half of 4 is 2.

Decimals

la décimale   tenth, decimal   **le centésimal**   hundredth

Arithmetical Signs

+ **et, plus**	**addition**	$2 + 2 = 4$	**Deux plus deux font quatre.**
− **moins**	**soustraction**	$8 - 7 = 1$	**Huit moins sept font un.**
× **multiplié par**	**multiplication**	$2 \times 3 = 6$	**Deux multiplié par trois font six.**
÷ **divisé par**	**division**	$6 \div 3 = 2$	**Six divisé par trois font deux.**

additionner   to add   **multiplier**   to multiply
soustraire   to subtract   **diviser**   to divide

Dimensions

Nouns	Adjectives
la hauteur height	**haut,-e** high, tall
la longueur length	**long, longue** long
la largeur width	**large** wide
la profondeur depth	**profond,-e** deep
l'épaisseur (*f.*) thickness	**épais,-se** thick

Avoir is often used to express dimensions.

La Tour Eiffel a trois cents mètres de haut.	The Eiffel Tower is 300 meters high.
La Loire a mille douze kilomètres de long.	The Loire river is 1,012 kilometers long.
Ce bifteck a trois centimètres d'épaisseur.	This steak is 3 centimeters thick.

Être de is also used to express dimensions.

La profondeur de ce puits est de trente mètres.	The depth of this well is 30 meters.
La largeur de ce paquet est de 75 centimètres.	The width of this package is 75 centimeters.

To tell someone's height, the verb *mesurer* is used. *Faire* can also be used.

Marc mesure un mètre quatre-vingt.	Marc is 1 m. 80 tall.
Ce meuble fait bien trois mètres.	This piece of furniture is at least three meters high.

Units of Measure, Metric System

l'hectare (*m.*)	hectare	(about 2 1/2 acres)
le kilo (kilogramme)	kilogram	(2.2 pounds)
le mètre	meter	(39.37 inches)
le kilomètre	kilometer	(about 5/8 of a mile)
le centimètre	centimeter	(0.39 inches)
le litre	liter	(a little over a quart)
la tonne	ton	(200 kilos)

Other Units of Measurement

le pouce	inch		**la pinte**	pint
le pied	foot		**le gallon**	gallon
le yard	yard		**la livre**	pound
le mille	mile			

Geometrical Terms

Surfaces planes:

la ligne	line		**le rectangle**	rectangle
l'angle (*m.*)	angle		**l'hexagone (*m.*)**	hexagon
l'angle droit (*m.*)	right angle		**le cercle**	circle
le triangle	triangle		**le diamètre**	diameter
le carré	square		**le rayon**	radius

Solids:

le cube   cube
le cylindre   cylinder
la sphère   sphere
l'hémisphère (*m.*)   hemisphere

la pyramide   pyramid
le cône   cone
le prisme   prism

29. Letters

Parts of a Letter

l'en-tête(*m.*)   heading
la vedette   name and address
l'appel (*m.*)   salutation
la date   date
l'objet (*m.*)   subject
le corps de la lettre   body of the letter
la référence   reference
la signature   signature

la formule de salutations   salutation (end)
la pièce jointe (P.J.) (pièces
   jointes)   enclosures
le code postal   zip code
CEDEX (Courrier d'entreprise à
   Distribution Exceptionnelle)   Business M
Boîte Postale   P.O. box

Heading

Lyon, le 5 avril 1983
New York, le 1er janvier 1983

Dakar, le 6 juin 1984
Montréal, le 30 septembre 1984

Address

Madame Solange Delhorme
6, rue Vendôme
22000 Grenoble
France

Monsieur le Directeur
Peugeot S.A.
58, avenue Général de Gaulle
69002 Lyon   France

Salutations

Business Letters

Monsieur, Sir:, Dear Sir:
Messieurs, Sirs:, Dear Sirs:
Madame et chère cliente,
   Madam and dear customer:

For more formal letters

Monsieur le Président, Mr. President:
Cher Maître, (to a lawyer or a notary)
Madame la Directrice,
   (to a woman director)

NOTE: One uses *cher (chère)* only when one knows the person well. When you do not know whether the woman is married or not, use *Madame*.

Personal letters

Cher ami, Chère amie,
Cher Paul, Chère Virginie
Mon cher cousin, Ma chère cousine
Ma chère petite Brigitte,

Dear friend,
Dear Paul, Dear Virginia,
Dear cousin,
Dear little Brigitte,

Ending

Formal or business letters

Je vous prie d'agréer (Veuillez recevoir), monsieur (madame, mademoiselle), l'expression de mes (nos) sentiments dévoués (distingués, respecteux).	Literally: Please accept, Sir (Madam, Miss, or Ms.), the expression of my (our) devoted (distinguished, respectful) sentiments.

Personal letters

Amitiés	With friendship,
Affectueusement,	Affectionately,
Ton copain,	Your pal,
Ton amie,	Your friend,
Bons baisers,	Affectionate kisses,
Je t'embrasse,	I kiss you,
A bientôt le plaisir de te lire (voir, parler)	I hope to have the pleasure soon to hear from (see, speak to) you.

Abbreviations

M.	monsieur	Mr.
Mme	madame	Mrs.
Mlle	mademoiselle	Miss or Ms.
MM.	messieurs	gentlemen, sirs
C.V.	curriculum vitae	résumé
C.C.P.	Compte chèque postal	postal bank account
Cie	compagnie	company
c.c.	copie conforme	carbon copy
P.J.	pièces jointes	enclosures
P.S.	postscriptum	postscript (P.S.)
P.-D.G.	Président-directeur général	Chairman and president
P.T.T.	Postes, télégraphes et téléphone	Postal, telegraph and telephone services
S.A.	société anonyme	incorporated company
S.A.R.L.	société anonyme à responsabilité limitée	limited liability company
R.S.V.P.	réponse, s'il vous plaît	please reply
	retournez, s'il vous plaît	please return
Ref.	Références	references
S.V.P.	s'il vous plaît	please

30. Idioms and Expressions

A

à bas. . .!   down with . . .!
à bientôt   see you soon
d'abord   at first
à cause de   because of
d'accord   agreed, OK
à droite   to the right
à l'envers   inside out
à la française   the French way
à gauche   to the left
à l'heure   on time
à la légère   lightly
à la longue   in the long run
à la maison   at home
à la mode   in fashion
à mi-temps   part-time
à nouveau   again
à part   aside
à peine   hardly
à plein temps   full-time
à peu près   nearly, approximately
à temps   on time
à tort ou à raison   rightly or wrongly
A vos souhaits!   God bless you!
aller bien   to be well
aller chez soi   to go home
aller mal   to not feel well
aller mieux   to feel better
Allons-y!   Let's go!
allumer la télé   to turn on the TV
au courant (de)   informed (about)
avoir l'air (de) + *inf*   to seem to
avoir l'air (de) + *noun*   to look like
avoir. . .ans   to be. . .years old
avoir besoin (de)   to need
avoir de la chance   to be lucky
avoir chaud   to be warm, hot
avoir confiance en   to have confidence in
avoir envie (de)   to want
avoir faim   to be hungry
avoir froid   to be cold
avoir hâte (de)   to be anxious to
avoir l'intention (de)   to intend
avoir lieu   to take place
avoir mal   to hurt
avoir le mal du pays   to be homesick

en avoir marre   to be fed up
avoir de la peine   to suffer, to be hurt
avoir peur (de)   to be afraid (of)
avoir raison   to be right
avoir soif   to be thirsty
avoir sommeil   to be sleepy
avoir tort   to be wrong
à voix basse   softly
à voix haute   loudly

B

bas:en bas   downstairs
bien de   a lot of
bien des   many
bien sûr!   of course!
bienvenue!   welcome!
bon anniversaire!   happy birthday!
bon courage!   have courage!
bon marché   inexpensive, reasonably priced
bonne année!   happy New Year!
bonne chance!   good luck!

C

chic, alors!   great!
ci-inclus   enclosed
ci-joint   enclosed
Comment ça se fait?   How come?
s'y connaître   to be an expert in, to know all about
contre: par contre   on the other hand
le coucher du soleil   sundown
le coup de chance   stroke of luck
le coup de fil   telephone call
le coup d'œil   glance

D

se débrouiller   to manage, to work things out
défense de. . .   it's forbidden to. . .
depuis longtemps   for a long time
dieu: mon dieu!   good heavens!
dire du mal (de)   to talk ill (of)
dis donc!   say!
donner à manger   to feed
se donner du mal   to go out of one's way

E

l'emploi du temps   schedule
en face de   opposite
en marche   in motion
entendre dire (que)   to hear (that)
entendre parler (de)   to hear (of)
entendu!   all right!
être de bonne humeur   to be in a good mood
être en train (de)   to be doing (something)
exemple: par exemple   for example

F

faire: s'en faire   to worry
faire attention   to be careful, to pay attention
faire de l'autostop   to hitchhike
faire du bricolage   to putter, to tinker
faire comme chez soi   to feel at home
faire confiance à   to trust (someone)
faire des courses   to go shopping
faire la cuisine   to cook
faire faire   to have something done
faire la lessive   to do the laundry
se faire mal   to get hurt
faire mal (à)   to hurt someone (physically)
faire sa médecine (son droit)   to study medicine (law)
faire le ménage   to do housework
faire de la peine (à)   to hurt someone's feelings
faire peur   to frighten
faire une promenade   to take a walk
faire la queue   to stand in line
faire réparer   to have (something) repaired
faire le repassage   to do the ironing
faire semblant (de)   to pretend (to)
faire du sport   to go in for sports
faire la vaisselle   to do the dishes
faire venir   to send for
faire un voyage   to take a trip
faute: sans faute   without fail
ficher: s'en ficher   not to care
fois: deux fois   twice
fois: pour la première fois   for the first time
fois: une fois   once
faut: comme il faut   properly
faut: ce qu'il te (vous) faut   what you need

G

grâce à   thanks to

H

d'habitude   usually, habitually
hasard: par hasard   by chance
haut: en haut   upstairs

I

ici: par ici   this way
n'importe   no matter
n'importe comment   no matter how
n'importe où   no matter where
n'importe quand   no matter when
n'importe qui   no matter who
n'importe quoi   no matter what
à l'instant   immediately, a moment ago

J

jeter un coup d'œil (sur)   to glance (at)
jouer à   to play (a sport)
jouer de   to play (a musical instrument)
le jour de congé   day off
jusqu'à   up to, as far as

L

là-bas   over there
le lever du soleil   sunrise

M

la machine à calculer   calculator
la machine à coudre   sewing machine
la machine à laver le linge   washing machine
manquer de (+ *noun*)   to be missing, to lack
manquer de (+ *inf.*)   to fail to, to come near to
marcher bien   to be in good order
marcher mal   to be out of condition
mettre de côté   to put aside, to save
mettre la table   to set the table
mettre la radio   to turn on the radio
mieux vaut   it's better to
mourir de faim   to starve
mourir de rire   to die laughing

N

n'est-ce pas?   is it not so?

O

l'offre d'emploi (*m.*) want ad
ouf! exclamation of relief

P

en panne out of order
se passer de to live without
passer le temps to spend time
peu importe never mind
pouvoir: n'en pouvoir plus to be
    exhausted
prendre soin de to take care of
prendre son temps to take one's time
prière de (verbe) please (verb)

Q

quand même even so, just the same
Qu'est-ce que c'est? What is it?
Qu'est-ce qui arrive? What's
    happening?
Qu'est-ce qu'il y a? What's the matter?
Qu'est-ce qui se passe? What is
    happening?
Qu'est-ce qui s'est passé? What
    happened?
Qu'est-ce qu'il te prend? What has
    come over you?
Quelle barbe! What a bore!

R

se rendre compte de/que to take into
    account, to realize
en retard late

S

sain et sauf safe and sound
sens: le bon sens common sense
sens dessus dessous upside down
se sentir bien to feel well
serrer la main to shake hands
tout(e) seul(e) all alone
sortir: s'en sortir to pull through, to
    get by

suivre un conseil to follow advice
suivre un cours to take a course

T

tant de so many, so much
tel quel just as it is, in the same
    condition
de temps en temps from time to time
tenir à to insist, to be bent on doing
    something
tenir compte de to take into account
tenir de to take after, resemble
tiens! why! well! look here!
tout à l'heure a little later
tout d'abord first of all
tout droit straight ahead
tout d'un coup all of a sudden
tous les deux the two of us, together
tout le monde everybody
tout près (de) very close (to)

U

l'un d'entre eux one of them
d'urgence urgently, immediately

V

vacances: les grandes
    vacances summer vacation
valoir le coup to be worthwhile
valoir mieux to be better
valoir la peine to be worthwhile, to be
    worth the trouble
vive. . .! long live. . .!
vouloir dire to mean
en vouloir à to have a grudge against,
    be resentful

Y

y compris included

Z

zut, alors! darn!

31. Vocabulary Lists

French-Speaking Countries

le pays	country	la capitale	capital
la France	France	Paris	Paris
la Belgique	Belgium	Bruxelles	Brussels
le Canada (Québec)	Canada (Quebec)	Québec	Quebec (capital of province of Quebec)
le Luxembourg	Luxembourg	Luxembourg	Luxembourg
la Suisse	Switzerland	Berne	Bern

Les Départements d'outre-mer ("DOM's")

(Overseas departments, having the same status as a department in France.)

le département	political division of France	la préfecture capital of department
la Guadeloupe	Guadeloupe	Pointe-à-Pitre
la Guyane française	French Guyana	Cayenne
la Martinique	Martinique	Fort-de-France
Saint-Martin	French Saint-Martin	Philipsburg

Les Territoires d'outre-mer

(Overseas territories)

le territoire	territory	la capitale	capital
la Nouvelle-Calédonie	New Caledonia	Nouméa	
la Polynésie	French Polynesia	Papeete	
la Réunion	Reunion	Saint-Denis	

Countries Where French Is Spoken as an Official Language

Pays		Capitale
le Bénin	Benin	Porto-Novo
le Burundi	Burundi	Usumbura
le Cameroun	Cameroon	Yaoundé
le Congo	Congo	Brazzaville
la Côte d'Ivoire	Ivory Coast	Abidjan
le Gabon	Gabon	Libreville
la Guinée	Guinea	Conakry
Haïti	Haiti	Port-au-Prince
la Haute-Volta	Upper Volta	Ouagadougou
le Laos	Laos	Vientiane
Madagascar	Madagascar	Tananarive

le Mali	Mali	Bamako
la Mauritanie	Mauritania	Nouakchott
le Niger	Niger	Niamey
la République Centrafricaine	Central African Republic	Bangui
la Ruanda	Rwanda	Kigali
le Sénégal	Senegal	Dakar
le Tchad	Chad	Ndjamena
le Togo	Togo	Lomé
la Zaire	Zaire	Kinshasa

Countries Where French Is Spoken as a Second Language

l'Algérie	Algeria	Alger
le Maroc	Morocco	Rabat
la Tunisie	Tunisia	Tunis

Commonly Used Words and Phrases

Current Expressions

Bonjour! Good morning! Good day!
Bonsoir! Good evening!
Bonne nuit! Good night!
Salut! Hi!
Comment allez-vous? How are you?
Comment vas-tu? How are you?
Ça va? Ça va. How's it going? OK.
Bien, très bien. Well, very well.
Pas mal, merci. Not bad, thank you.
Au revoir! Good-bye!
A bientôt! See you soon!
A demain! See you tomorrow!
A lundi! See you Monday!
D'accord! OK!

monsieur Mr., sir
madame Mrs., lady
mademoiselle Miss, Ms., young lady
Oui, madame! Yes, ma'am!
Non, monsieur! No, sir!
s'il vous plaît please
Merci beaucoup! Thank you very
  much!
Je vous en prie.
De rien. } You're welcome.
Il n'y a pas de quoi.
Excusez-moi. Excuse me, I'm sorry.
Je m'excuse. I'm sorry.
Pardon. I beg your pardon.

Nationalities and Languages

allemand — l'allemand (*m.*) German

anglais — l'anglais (*m.*) English
chinois — le chinois Chinese
espagnol — l'espagnol (*m.*) Spanish
français — le français French
italien — l'italien (*m.*) Italian
japonais — le japonais Japanese
portugais — le portugais Portuguese
russe — le russe Russian

Commonly Used Items

le cahier (d'exercices) notebook
  (workbook)
la carte map
la corbeille à papiers wastepaper
  basket
la craie chalk
le crayon pencil
l'encre (*f.*) ink
l'enveloppe (*f.*) envelope
l'examen (*m.*) exam, test
la gomme eraser
la lettre letter
le livre book
le papier paper
le stylo pen
le tableau chalkboard
le timbre stamp

Beverages

la bière beer
la boisson drink, beverage
le café coffee
le café crème coffee with cream

le chocolat   hot chocolate
le cidre   cider
l'eau (f.)   water
l'eau minérale (f.)   mineral water
la glace   ice
le jus d'orange   orange juice
le jus de pamplemousse   grapefruit
   juice
le lait   milk
la limonade   lemon soda
le thé   tea
le vin   wine

Food

les aliments (m.)   food
le beurre   butter
le biscuit   cracker
le bonbon   candy
les conserves (f.)   canned goods
le croissant   crescent roll
le fromage   cheese
le gâteau   cake
la glace   ice cream
l'huile (f.)   oil
le macaroni   macaroni
le miel   honey
la moutarde   mustard
la nouille   noodle
le pain   bread
le pâté   pâté
le pâté de foie gras   goose liver pâté
le petit gâteau   cookie
le petit pain   roll
le poivre   pepper
le riz   rice
le sandwich   sandwich
le sel   salt
le spaghetti   spaghetti
le sucre   sugar
la tarte   pie
le vinaigre   vinegar

Meats

l'agneau (m.)   lamb
le bifteck   steak
le bœuf   beef
la côtelette   cutlet, chop
l'escalope (f.)   cutlet
le foie   liver
le gigot   leg of lamb
le jambon   ham
le lard   bacon
le mouton   lamb
le porc   pork

le rognon   kidney
le rosbif   roast beef
la saucisse   sausage
le saucisson   salami
le veau   veal

Fowl

le canard   duck
la dinde   turkey
l'oie (f.)   goose
le poulet   chicken
la volaille   fowl

Fish

la crevette   shrimp
l'huître (f.)   oyster
la langouste   lobster
la morue   cod
la moule   mussel
la palourde   clam
le poisson   fish
la sardine   sardine
le saumon   salmon
le thon   tuna
la truite   trout

Vegetables

l'ail (m.)   garlic
l'artichaut (m.)   artichoke
l'asperge (f.)   asparagus
la carotte   carrot
le céleri   celery
le chou   cabbage
le chou-fleur   cauliflower
l'épinard (m.)   spinach
le haricot vert   green bean
la laitue   lettuce
le légume   vegetable
le maïs   corn
l'oignon (m.)   onion
l'olive (f.)   olive
le persil   parsley
le petit pois   pea
le poireau   leek
le poivron   pepper
la pomme de terre   potato
le radis   radish
la tomate   tomato

Fruits and Nuts

l'abricot (m.)   apricot
l'airelle (f.)   cranberry

l'amande (*f.*)   almond
l'ananas (*m.*)   pineapple
l'avocat (*m.*)   avocado
la banane   banana
la cacahuète   peanut
la cerise   cherry
le citron   lemon
la date   date
la figue   fig
la fraise   strawberry
la framboise   raspberry
le fruit   fruit
le melon   melon, cantaloupe
la mûre   blackberry
la myrtille   blueberry
la noisette   hazelnut
la noix   walnut
l'orange (*f.*)   orange
le pamplemousse   grapefruit
la pastèque   watermelon
la pêche   peach
la poire   pear
la pomme   apple
la prune   plum
le raisin   grape

Meals

le casse-croûte   heavy snack
le déjeuner   lunch (midday meal)
le dîner   dinner (evening meal)
le goûter   afternoon snack (for children)
le petit déjeuner   breakfast
le pique-nique   picnic
le repas   meal
le souper   supper (late evening)

Menu

la (sauce) béarnaise   hot sauce with butter, egg yolks, shallots, and tarragon
la bouillabaisse   fish soup
le civet de lapin   rabbit stew
le croûton   crouton
le dessert   dessert
l'entrée (*f.*)   first course
les escargots (*m.*)   snails
les fruits de mer (*m.*)   seafood
la (sauce) hollandaise   hot sauce with butter, egg yolks, and lemon
le hors d'œuvre   hors d'oeuvre
la mayonnaise   mayonnaise

la note   check (in restaurant)
l'œuf dur (*m.*)   hard-boiled egg
l'omelette (*f.*)   omelet
le plat du jour   the special (of the day)
le plateau de fromages   cheese tray
le potage   thick soup
le pourboire   tip
la quiche   quiche
le ragoût   meat stew
le rôti   roast
la salade   salad
la sauce (de salade)   dressing
la soupe   soup
la vinaigrette   dressing of mustard, vinegar, and oil

bleu   rare
saignant   medium rare
à point   well done
à la carte   separate price for each dish
au jus   with natural juices
au gratin   broiled with topping of cheese
en brochette   on a skewer
en croûte   in a pastry shell
en purée   mashed
le cordon bleu   excellent cook
le chef de cuisine   chef

The Table

l'assiette (*f.*)   plate
la cafetière   coffeepot
la corbeille à pain   breadbasket
le couteau   knife
la cuillère (à soupe)   (soup)spoon
la fourchette   fork
la nappe   tablecloth
le plat   (serving) dish
le plateau   tray
le poivrier   pepper mill
la salière   saltshaker
le sucrier   sugar bowl
la théière   teapot
la vaisselle   dishes
le verre   glass

mettre le couvert   to set the table
débarrasser la table   to clear the table

The Human Body

la barbe   beard
la bouche   mouth

le bras arm
les cheveux (*m.*) hair
la cheville ankle
le cil eyelash
le cœur heart
le coude elbow
la dent tooth
le doigt finger
le doigt de pied toe
le dos back
l'épaule (*f.*) shoulder
l'estomac (*m.*) stomach
la figure face
le foie liver
le front forehead
le genou knee
la gorge throat
la jambe leg
la joue cheek
la langue tongue
la lèvre lip
la main hand
le menton chin
la moustache mustache
le nez nose
l'œil (*m.*) (les yeux) eye
l'ongle (*m.*) nail
l'oreille (*f.*) ear
la paupière eyelid
la peau skin
le pied foot
le poignet wrist
la poitrine chest
le sourcil eyebrow
la tête head
le visage face

The Family and Relatives

l'arrière-grand-mère (*f.*) great-grandmother
l'arrière-grand-père (*m.*) great-grandfather
le beau-fils stepson
le beau-frère brother-in-law
le beau-père father-in-law, stepfather
la belle-fille stepdaughter, daughter-in-law
la belle-mère mother-in-law, stepmother
la belle-sœur sister-in-law
la bru daughter-in-law
le cousin, la cousine cousin
l'enfant (*m. & f.*) child

l'époux, l'épouse spouse
la famille family
la femme wife
la fille daughter
le fils son
le frère brother
le gendre son-in-law
la grand-mère grandmother
le grand-père grandfather
le mari husband
la mère mother
le neveu nephew
la nièce niece
l'oncle (*m.*) uncle
les parents (*m.*) parents, relatives
le père father
la petite-fille granddaughter
le petit-fils grandson
les petits-enfants (*m.*) grandchildren
la sœur sister
la tante aunt

The House

l'appartement (*m.*) apartment
l'ascenseur (*m.*) elevator
la chambre bedroom
la cheminée chimney, fireplace
le corridor corridor
la cuisine kitchen
l'entrée (*f.*) foyer
l'escalier (*m.*) stairs
la fenêtre window
le gratte-ciel skyscraper
l'immeuble (*m.*) apartment building
la maison house
le mur wall
la pièce room
le placard closet, cupboard
le plafond ceiling
le plancher floor
la porte-fenêtre French window
le premier (étage) second floor
le rez-de-chaussée first (main) floor
la salle à manger dining room
la salle de bains bathroom
la salle de séjour combination living and dining room
le salon living room
le toit roof

Furniture

l'armoire (*f.*) wardrobe

le buffet china cabinet
le bureau desk
la chaise chair
la commode dresser
la cuisinière stove
le fauteuil armchair
la lampe lamp
le lit bed
le lustre chandelier
le meuble furniture
la moquette carpeting
le réfrigérateur refrigerator
le rideau curtain
la table table
le tableau painting
le tapis rug

The Bed

faire le lit to make the bed
la couverture blanket
le dessus-de-lit bedspread
le drap sheet
l'édredon (m.) comforter
le matelas mattress
l'oreiller (m.) pillow
la taie d'oreiller pillowcase

Toilet Articles

la brosse brush
la brosse à dents toothbrush
les ciseaux scissors
la crème à raser shaving cream
la crème solaire suntan lotion
le dentifrice toothpaste
l'eau de Cologne (f.) cologne
la lime à ongles nail file
le miroir mirror
le parfum perfume
le peigne comb
la poudre powder
le rasoir razor
le rouge à lèvres lipstick
le savon soap
la serviette de toilette towel
le shampooing shampoo

Clothing

la blouse blouse
le blouson windbreaker
la ceinture belt
le chapeau hat

la chaussette sock
la chaussure shoe
la chemise shirt
le col collar
le collant pantyhose
le complet suit
la cravate necktie
le gant glove
l'imperméable (m.) raincoat
le jean jeans
la jupe skirt
la lingerie lingerie
le manteau coat
la mode fashion
le mouchoir handkerchief
le pantalon pants, slacks
la pantoufle slipper
le parapluie umbrella
le pardessus overcoat
le portefeuille wallet
le pull-over sweater
le pyjama pyjamas
la robe dress
la robe de chambre robe
le sac purse
le short shorts
les tennis (m.) sneakers
le T-shirt T-shirt
la veste jacket
le vêtement article of clothing

s'habiller to get dressed
se déshabiller to get undressed
porter to wear

Animals

l'agneau (m.) lamb
l'aigle (m.) eagle
l'âne (m.) donkey
l'animal (m.) animal
la baleine whale
le bœuf ox
le chameau camel
le chat cat
le cheval horse
la chèvre goat
le chien dog
la colombe dove
le coq rooster
le crapaud toad
le crocodile crocodile
le daim deer
l'écureuil (m.) squirrel

l'éléphant (*m.*)　elephant
la girafe　giraffe
la grenouille　frog
le lapin　rabbit
le lion　lion
le loup　wolf
le mouton　sheep
la mule　mule
l'oiseau (*m.*)　bird
l'ours (*m.*)　bear
le perroquet　parrot
le pigeon　pigeon
le poisson　fish
la poule　hen
le renard　fox
le requin　shark
le serpent　snake
le singe　monkey
la souris　mouse
le taureau　bull
le tigre　tiger
la tortue　turtle
la vache　cow
le veau　calf

Insects

l'abeille (*f.*)　bee
l'araignée (*f.*)　spider
le cafard　cockroach
la coccinelle　ladybug
la fourmi　ant
l'insecte (*m.*)　insect
le mille-pattes　centipede
la mite　moth
la mouche　fly
le moustique　mosquito
le papillon　butterfly
la puce　flea
la sauterelle　grasshopper
le ver　worm

The Garden

le buisson　bush
le chrysanthème　chrysanthemum
la fleur　flower
le gazon　lawn
le géranium　geranium
l'herbe (*f.*)　grass
le jardin　garden
le lilas　lilac
le lis　lily
la marguerite　daisy

le muguet　lily of the valley
l'œillet (*m.*)　carnation
l'orchidée (*f.*)　orchid
la pensée　pansy
la rose　rose
la tulipe　tulip

tondre le gazon　to mow the lawn
planter　to plant
arroser　to water

Trees

l'arbre (*m.*)　tree
le bouleau　birch
le cèdre　cedar
le chêne　oak
l'érable (*m.*)　maple
le frêne　ash
le marronier　chestnut
le palmier　palm tree
le peuplier　poplar
le pin　pine tree
le platane　plane-tree
le sapin　fir
le saule pleureur　weeping willow

Studies

l'algèbre (*f.*)　algebra
la biologie　biology
la botanique　botany
la chimie　chemistry
la comptabilité　accounting
le cours　class, course
le dessin　drawing
la géographie　geography
la géométrie　geometry
la gym(nastique)　physical education
l'histoire (*f.*)　history
l'informatique (*m.*)　computer science,
　　data processing
la langue étrangère　foreign language
les maths (mathématiques)　math
la matière　school subject
la musique　music
la peinture　painting
la physique　physics
les sciences　science
la sténographie　shorthand
la zoologie　zoology

passer un examen　to take an exam
réussir à un examen　to pass an exam

The Office

le classeur   filing cabinet
le dossier   file
la machine à calculer   adding machine, calculator
la machine à écrire   typewriter
l'ordinateur (*m.*)   computer

taper à la machine   to type
classer   to file
dicter   to dictate

The City

l'aéroport (*m.*)   airport
l'avenue (*f.*)   avenue
le boulevard   boulevard
le carrefour   intersection
le cimetière   cemetery
la circulation   traffic
l'embouteillage (*m.*)   traffic jam
le feu rouge   red light
le feu vert   green light
la gare   train station
l'immeuble   apartment building
le métro   subway
le monument   monument
le parc   park
la petite ville   town
la place   square
le piéton   pedestrian
le pont   bridge
le quai   dock, pier, street along a river
le quartier   city district, quarter
la rue   street
le sens interdit   wrong way
le sens unique   one way (street)
le square   square (with garden)
le stade   stadium
le trottoir   sidewalk
la ville   city

Buildings

la banque   bank
le bâtiment   building
la bibliothèque   library
le café   café
la cathédrale   cathedral
le château   castle
le cinéma   movie theater
le commissariat de police   police station

l'école (*f.*)   school
l'église (*f.*)   church
la fabrique   factory
l'hôpital (*m.*)   hospital
l'hôtel (*m.*)   hotel
l'hôtel de ville (*m.*)   city hall
la mairie   town hall
le musée   museum
l'opéra (*m.*)   opera house
le palais   palace
la poste   post office
la prison   jail
la synagogue   synagogue
le théâtre   theater

Stores and Shops

la bijouterie   jewelry store
la blanchisserie   laundromat
la boucherie   butcher shop
la boulangerie   bakery
la boutique   boutique
la charcuterie   pork-butcher shop
la confiserie   candy store
la cordonnerie   shoe repair shop
la crémerie   dairy
la devanture   storefront
l'épicerie (*f.*)   grocery store
le grand magasin   department store
la laiterie   dairy
la librairie   bookstore
le magasin   shop, store
le marchand de chaussures   shoe store
le marchand de journaux   newspaper stand
le merchand de primeurs   fruit and vegetable store
le marchand de vins   liquor store
le marché   market
la papeterie   stationery store
la pâtisserie   pastry shop
la pharmacie   pharmacy
la poissonnerie   fish market
la quincaillerie   hardware store
le restaurant   restaurant
le supermarché   supermarket
le tailleur   tailor shop
la teinturerie   dry cleaner

faire du lèche-vitrine   to go window-shopping

Transportation

l'autobus (*m.*) city bus
l'autocar (*m.*) intercity bus
l'avion (*m.*) plane
le bateau ship, boat
la bicyclette bicycle
le camion truck
l'hélicoptère (*m.*) helicopter
le jet jet
le métro subway
la mobylette moped
la motocyclette motorcycle
le T.G.V. (train à grande
    vitesse) high-speed train
le taxi taxi
le téléférique cable car
le train train
le voilier sailboat
la voiture car

Journey, Trip

les bagages (*m.*) luggage
le billet ticket
le billet aller-retour round-trip ticket
le bureau de voyages travel agency
la douane customs
l'horaire (*m.*) schedule
le passeport passport
la place seat
le porteur porter
la réservation reservation
la valise suitcase

enregistrer les bagages to check the
    luggage
Bon voyage! Have a good trip!

Professions and Trades

l'acteur (*m.*) actor
l'actrice (*f.*) actress
l'agent de police (*m.*) policeman
l'architecte (*m. & f.*) architect
l'avocat(e) lawyer
le (la) banquier(ère) banker
le (la) boucher(ère) butcher
le (la) boulanger(ère) baker
le charpentier carpenter
le chauffeur de taxi taxi driver
le (la) coiffeur(euse) hairdresser
le (la) commerçant(e) merchant

le (la) comptable accountant
le (la) dentiste dentist
le docteur doctor
l'écrivain (*m.*) writer
l'électricien(ne) electrician
le facteur letter carrier
le (la) fermier(ère) farmer
le (la) fleuriste florist
l'infirmier(ère) nurse
l'ingénieur (*m.*) engineer
l'instituteur, l'institutrice teacher
le (la) journaliste journalist
le juge judge
le (la) mécanicien(ne) mechanic
le (la) musicien(ne) musician
l'ouvrier(ère) worker
le paysan peasant
le (la) peintre painter
le (la) pharmacien(ne) pharmacist
le (la) photographe photographer
le (la) pilote pilot
le plombier plumber
le prêtre priest
le professeur professor, teacher
le (la) secrétaire secretary
le soldat (la femme soldat) soldier
le (la) vendeur(euse) salesperson
le (la) voyageur(euse) de
    commerce traveling salesperson

Governmental Titles

le président president
le vice président vice-president
le premier ministre prime minister
le gouverneur governor
le préfet head of *département*
    (administrative division in France)
le sous-préfet assistant to *préfet*
le maire mayor

Metals

l'acier (*m.*) steel
l'aluminium (*m.*) aluminum
l'argent (*m.*) silver
le bronze bronze
le cuivre copper
l'étain (*m.*) tin, pewter
le fer iron
le laiton brass
l'or (*m.*) gold
le platine platinum

le plomb   lead
le zinc   zinc

Materials

le bois   wood
la brique   brick
le caoutchouc   rubber
le ciment   cement
le coton   cotton
la laine   wool
le marbre   marble
le plâtre   plaster
la soie   silk
la toile   linen
la tuile   tile
le verre   glass

Geography

la baie   bay
le bois   wood
la colline   hill
le continent   continent
la côte   coast
le désert   desert
la dune   dune
l'étang (m.)   pond
le fleuve   large river
la forêt   forest
l'hémisphère (f.)   hemisphere
l'île (f.)   island
le lac   lake
le marécage   swamp
la mer   sea
la montagne   mountain
l'océan (m.)   ocean
la péninsule   peninsula
le pic   peak
la plage   beach
la plaine   plain
le plateau   plateau
la rivière   small river
la terre   earth
la vallée   valley

Sports

la balle   small ball (tennis)
le ballon   large ball (football, soccer)
le base-ball   baseball
le basket-ball   basketball
les boules   bowling (French)
la boxe   boxing

la course   race
l'entraînement (faire de)   practice (to practice)
l'équipe (f.)   team
le football (le foot)   soccer
le footing   walking
le golf   golf
le hockey   hockey
le jeu   game
le jogging   jogging
la lutte   wrestling
le match   match
la natation   swimming
le patin à glace   ice skating
le patin à roulettes   roller skating
le ping-pong   Ping-Pong
le ski   skiing
le ski nautique   water skiing
le sport   sport
le tennis   tennis
le vol à voile   gliding

The Car

l'accélérateur (m.)   accelerator
l'air (m.)   air
la batterie   battery
le changement de vitesse   gears, transmission
le coffre   trunk
l'essence (f.)   gasoline
l'essuie-glace (m.)   windshield wiper
le frein   brake
le garage   garage
la graisse   grease
l'huile (f.)   oil
le moteur   engine
la panne   breakdown
le pare-brise   windshield
le pneu   tire
le pneu crevé   flat tire
le pneu de rechange   spare tire
le réservoir   tank
le rétroviseur   driving mirror
la roue   wheel
la station d'essence   gas station
la vitesse   speed
la voiture   car
le volant   steering wheel

conduire   to drive
tomber en panne   to have a breakdown

Holidays

*Noël   Christmas
*Le Nouvel an   New Year's Day
 Le Mardi gras   Fat Tuesday (Shrove
    Tuesday)
 La Semaine sainte   Holy Week
 Le Vendredi saint   Good Friday
*Pâques   Easter
*La Pentecôte   Whitsunday
*Le Premier mai (Fête du
    travail)   May 1st (French Labor
    Day)
*Le 14 juillet (fête nationale)   July
    14th (Bastille Day)
*Le 15 août   Assumption Day
*Le 11 novembre   Veterans Day

*Official holidays in France.

Polite Phrases

Félicitations!   Congratulations!
Bonnes vacances!   Have a good
    vacation!
Joyeux Noël!   Merry Christmas!
Bonne Année!   Happy New Year!
Bonne chance!   Good luck!
Amusez-vous bien!   Have a good time!
Joyeux anniversaire!   Happy
    birthday!
Bonne fête!   Happy name day!
Merci.   Thank you.

Index

Verb Index

This verb index will enable you to compare hundreds of commonly used verbs to the book's numerous verb tables. Each of the following groups of regular or irregular verbs provides the page numbers where the various verb tenses are discussed in the book. Each group is then followed by some of the most common verbs—and their definitions—that follow those patterns. By recognizing which verbs follow a certain pattern, you will greatly increase your vocabulary—all at a glance.

Regular Verbs

Regular verbs can be categorized into three major groups according to their infinitive form endings. These endings are -er, -ir, or -re.

-er Verbs

Regular -er verbs are conjugated in the same way as the verb *parler*. The various conjugations of *parler* can be found on the following pages:

infinitive, 6	*imparfait* (imperfect), 10
present, 7	*passé simple* (simple past), 11
imperative, 13	past participle; 16, 17
future, 11	present subjunctive, 23
conditional, 12	past subjunctive, 24

Some common -er verbs appear in the following list.

NOTE: Some verbs use the auxiliary *être* in compound tenses. This is indicated in parentheses. A few verbs use the auxiliary *avoir* when they are followed by a direct object, but use the auxiliary *être* when they are not followed by a direct object. This is also noted after the verb.

abandonner to abandon
abonner to subscribe
aborder to tackle, approach
abriter to give shelter
abuser to abuse
accentuer to accentuate
accepter to accept

accompagner to accompany
accorder to grant
accrocher to hang up
accuser to accuse
adapter to adapt
admirer to admire
adopter to adopt

adorer   to adore
adresser   to address
agréer   to accept
aider   to help
aimer   to love, like
ajouter   to add
allumer   to light, turn on
amuser   to amuse
apporter   to bring
apprécier   to appreciate
apprendre   to learn
arrêter   to stop, arrest
arriver   to arrive (aux. *être*)
assister   to attend
baisser   to lower
bavarder   to chat
blaguer   to kid, joke
blesser   to hurt
brancher   to plug in, connect
brosser   to brush
brûler   to burn
cacher   to hide
casser   to break
cesser   to cease
changer   to change
chanter   to sing
chauffer   to warm up
chercher   to look for
circuler   to circulate, move along
coiffer   to style (hair)
commander   to order
comparer   to compare
composer   to dial
confier   to entrust, confide
conseiller   to advise
consoler   to console
continuer   to continue
coucher   to put to bed
couper   to cut
créer   to create
crier   to shout, yell
cuisiner   to cook
danser   to dance
déchirer   to tear
décider   to decide
déclarer   to declare
déjeuner   to have lunch
demander   to ask
démontrer   to demonstrate
dépasser   to pass, exceed
déranger   to disturb
déshabiller   to undress

désirer   to desire
dessiner   to draw
détester   to detest
dîner   to have dinner
donner   to give
échapper   to avoid, escape
écouter   to listen
embêter   to annoy, bother
embrasser   to kiss
empêcher   to prevent
emprunter   to borrow
enseigner   to teach
entrer   to enter (aux. *être*)
épouser   to marry
étonner   to astonish, surprise
étudier   to study
éviter   to avoid
excuser   to excuse
expliquer   to explain
exprimer   to express
fâcher   to anger (someone)
féliciter   to congratulate
fermer   to close
fêter   to celebrate, party
fonder   to found
fumer   to smoke
gagner   to win
garder   to keep
gêner   to bother, embarrass
goûter   to taste
guider   to guide
habiller   to dress
habiter   to live, reside
hésiter   to hesitate
imaginer   to imagine
indiquer   to indicate
informer   to inform
insister   to insist
intéresser   to interest
interroger   to interrogate
inviter   to invite
jouer   to play
juger   to judge
jurer   to swear, vow
laisser   to let, leave (behind)
laver   to wash
louer   to praise
manquer   to miss, lack
monter   to go up, take up (aux. *être* or *avoir*)
montrer   to show
organiser   to organize

oser   to dare
oublier   to forget
pardonner   to forgive
parler   to speak
passer   to pass, spend (time), take (exam) (aux. *être* or *avoir*)
peigner   to comb
penser   to think
porter   to carry, wear
pousser   to push
préparer   to prepare
présenter   to present
prêter   to lend
prier   to beg, pray
proposer   to propose
quitter   to quit, leave
raconter   to tell
recommander   to recommend
reculer   to back up
refuser   to refuse
regarder   to look at, watch
regretter   to regret
remarquer   to notice
remercier   to thank
rencontrer   to meet
renseigner   to inform
rentrer   to go back, take back in (aux. *être* or *avoir*)
réparer   to repair
respecter   to respect
ressembler   to look like

rester   to stay (aux. *être*)
retourner   to return (somewhere), turn over (aux. *être* or *avoir*)
réveiller   to wake up
rêver   to dream
risquer   to risk
sauver   to save
sembler   to appear, seem
séparer   to separate
skier   to ski
songer   to think, ponder
sonner   to ring
souhaiter   to wish
supporter   to bear
télécopier   to fax
téléphoner   to telephone
terminer   to finish
tomber   to fall (aux. *être*)
toucher   to touch
tourner   to turn
tousser   to cough
travailler   to work
traverser   to cross
tromper   to deceive
trouver   to find
tuer   to kill
utiliser   to use
vérifier   to check
visiter   to visit
voler   to steal, fly
voter   to vote

-*ir* Verbs

Regular -*ir* verbs are conjugated in the same way as the verb *finir*. The various conjugations of *finir* can be found on the following pages:

infinitive, 6	*imparfait* (imperfect), 10
present, 8	*passé simple* (simple past), 11
imperative, 13	past participle; 16, 17
future, 11	present subjunctive, 23
conditional, 12	past subjunctive, 24

Some common -*ir* verbs appear in the following list:

abolir   to abolish
accomplir   to accomplish
agir   to act
agrandir   to enlarge

atterrir   to land
bâtir   to build
bénir   to bless
brunir   to tan

choisir   to choose
élargir   to widen
finir   to finish
grandir   to grow
grossir   to gain weight
guérir   to heal
investir   to invest
maigrir   to lose weight
mincir   to get slimmer
nourrir   to feed
obéir   to obey
pourrir   to rot
punir   to punish

raccourcir   to shorten
rajeunir   to feel younger, rejuvenate
ralentir   to slow down
réfléchir   to think over
remplir   to fill (up)
réunir   to gather
réussir   to succeed
rôtir   to roast
rougir   to blush
saisir   to seize
unir   to join
vieillir   to grow old

-re Verbs

Regular *-re* verbs are conjugated in the same way as the verb *vendre*. The various conjugations of *vendre* can be found on the following pages:

infinitive, 6	*imparfait* (imperfect), 10
present, 9	*passé simple* (simple past), 11
imperative, 13	past participle, 16
future, 11	present subjunctive, 23
conditional, 12	past subjunctive, 24

Some common *-re* verbs appear in the following list.

NOTE: Some verbs use the auxiliary *être* in compound tenses. This is noted in parentheses after the verb. A few verbs use the auxiliary *avoir* when followed by a direct object but use the auxiliary *être* when they are not followed by a direct object. This is also noted after the verb.

attendre   to wait
défendre   to defend, forbid
descendre   to go down, take down
   (aux. *être* or *avoir*)
entendre   to hear
fondre   to melt
mordre   to bite

perdre   to lose
rendre   to return, give back
répandre   to spill, spread
répondre   to answer
tendre   to stretch, extend
tondre   to mow
vendre   to sell

Irregular Verbs

There are various types of irregular verbs. Contrary to a regular verb, which is characterized by a stem and an ending that remains constant in a given conjugation, the stem of an irregular verb may change within a given conjugation and its endings are often unpredictable.

-*er* Verbs

The various conjugations of irregular -*er* verbs can be found on pages 31 and 32. The compound tenses for irregular -*er* verbs are conjugated the same as those for regular -*er* verbs, or they follow the conjugations of the verbs from which they are derived, such as *tourner/retourner*.

Stem-Changing Verbs with *Accent Grave* Added to Mute -*e*-

The following stem-changing verbs have regular -*er* verb endings, but the mute -*e*- of the verb stem gains an *accent grave* in some of the conjugated forms. They follow the same conjugation patterns as the verb *acheter*, which can be found on page 32. Some of these verbs are:

acheter to buy	**lever** to raise
achever to finish, complete	**mener** to lead (someone)
emmener to take away (someone)	**peser** to weigh
geler to freeze	**promener** to walk (someone)

Stem-Changing Verbs with *Accent Grave* Replacing *Accent Aigu*

These verbs have regular -*er* verb endings, but the *accent aigu* over the -*e*- of the verb stem is replaced by an *accent grave* in some of the conjugated forms. They are conjugated in the same way as the verb *préférer*, which can be found on page 32. Some of these verbs are:

céder to give in	**interpréter** to interpret
célébrer to celebrate	**posséder** to possess
compléter to complete	**préférer** to prefer
espérer to hope	**protéger** to protect
exagérer to exaggerate	**répéter** to repeat

Stem-Changing Verbs with *Cédille* Added

These verbs have regular -*er* verb endings, but the -*c*- of the verb stem gains a *cédille* in some of the conjugated forms. They follow the conjugation patterns of the verb *commencer*, which can be found on page 31. Some of these verbs are:

annoncer to announce	**menacer** to threaten
avancer to move forward	**placer** to place
commencer to start	**prononcer** to pronounce
effacer to erase	**remplacer** to replace
lancer to toss, throw	

Stem-Changing Verbs with -*e*- Added After -*g*- in the Stem

These verbs have regular -*er* verb endings, but a mute -*e*- is added to the verb stem in some of the conjugated forms. They follow the conjugation patterns of the verb *manger*, which can be found on page 31. Some of these verbs are:

arranger	to arrange	**manger**	to eat
bouger	to move	**nager**	to swim
changer	to change	**neiger**	to snow
corriger	to correct	**obliger**	to force, require
déranger	to disturb	**partager**	to share
exiger	to demand	**plonger**	to dive
infliger	to inflict	**voyager**	to travel

Stem-Changing Verbs with -*i*- Replacing -*y*- in the Stem

These verbs have regular -*er* verb endings, but the -*y*- of the stem becomes an -*i*- in some of the conjugated forms. Unless otherwise indicated, they follow the conjugation patterns of the verb *payer*, which can be found on page 32. Some of these verbs are:

employer	to use, employ	**essuyer**	to wipe, dry
ennuyer	to annoy, bore	**nettoyer**	to clean
envoyer/renvoyer	to send, send back, fire	**noyer**	to drown
essayer	to try	**payer**	to pay

-*ir* Verbs (Not -*iss*)

There are several patterns of conjugation for irregular -*ir* verbs. Their various conjugations can be found on the pages indicated next to each of the following verbs. The compound tenses for irregular -*ir* verbs are conjugated the same as those for regular -*ir* verbs, or they follow the conjugation patterns of the verbs from which they are derived, such as *dormir/endormir*. When a verb requires the use of the auxillary *être* in the compound tenses, this is noted in parentheses.

Irregular -*ir* Verbs Following the Conjugation Pattern of *Partir*

dormir	to sleep, 37	**ressentir**	to feel (pain or emotion), 40
endormir	to put to sleep, 37	**sentir**	to feel, smell; 40
mentir	to lie, 40	**servir**	to serve, 40
partir	to leave, 39 (aux. *être*)	**sortir**	to go out, 40 (aux. *être* or *avoir*)

Irregular -*ir* Verbs Following the Conjugation Pattern of *Ouvrir*

couvrir	to cover, 39	**ouvrir**	to open, 39
cueillir	to pick, 37	**recueillir**	to gather, collect; 37
découvrir	to discover, 39	**souffrir**	to suffer, 39
offrir	to offer, 39		

Irregular -*ir* Verbs Following the Conjugation Patterns of *Venir* and *Tenir*

devenir	to become, 42 (aux. *être*)	**tenir**	to hold, 42
obtenir	to obtain, 42	**venir**	to come, 41 (aux. *être*)
revenir	to come back, 42 (aux. *être*)		

Courir and *Mourir*

courir	to run, 36	**mourir** to die; 38, 39 (aux. *être*)

-*re* Verbs

The majority of -*re* verbs have some irregular forms in various tenses and modes. Most of them have an irregular past participle and subjunctive. The verbs listed below have at least some of these irregular forms. Their various conjugations can be found on the pages indicated next to each verb. When a verb requires the use of the auxiliary *être* in compound tenses, this is noted in parentheses.

comprendre	to understand, 40	**paraître**	to seem, appear; 36
conduire	to drive, 35	**peindre**	to paint, 36
connaître	to know, 36	**permettre**	to permit, allow; 38
croire	to believe, 36	**plaindre**	to pity, 36
décrire	to describe, 37	**plaire**	to please, 39
déplaire	to displease, 39	**prendre**	to take, 40
détruire	to destroy, 35	**promettre**	to promise, 38
dire	to say, tell; 37	**reconnaître**	to recognize, 36
disparaître	to disappear, 36	**rejoindre**	to join, meet; 36
écrire	to write, 37	**rire**	to laugh, 40
éteindre	to turn off, extinguish; 36	**suivre**	to follow, 41
faire	to do, make; 38	**surprendre**	to surprise, 40
inscrire	to enroll (someone), note; 37	**survivre**	to survive, 42
lire	to read, 38	**traduire**	to translate, 35
mettre	to put, put on; 38	**vivre**	to live, 42
naître	to be born (aux. *être*), 39		

-*oir* Verbs

The -*oir* verbs have some irregular forms, which can be found on the pages indicated next to each of the following verbs:

devoir	to have to, 37	**savoir**	to know, 40
pleuvoir	to rain, 44	**voir**	to see, 42
pouvoir	to be able to, 40	**vouloir**	to want, 42

Auxiliary Verbs

The verbs *avoir* and *être*, which have irregular patterns of conjugation, serve as auxiliary verbs in compound tenses such as the *passé composé*. These verbs can be found on pages 34 and 51. Similarly, various irregular conjugations of the verb *aller*, which serves as an auxiliary verb for the near future, can be found on pages 35 and 51.

aller to go   **être** to be
avoir to have

Reflexive or Pronominal Verbs

These verbs are used when the action reflects back to the person doing it: *Je me lave* (I wash myself). The reflexive verb conjugations depend on whether they are regular *-er*, *-ir*, or *-re* verbs or irregular verbs. What distinguishes a reflexive verb from a nonreflexive verb is that the verb is preceded by a reflexive pronoun (*me, te, se, nous,* or *vous*), which corresponds to the subject of the verb. Any verb that admits a direct or indirect object may be used reflexively: *laver/se laver* (to wash/to wash oneself).

NOTE: All verbs used reflexively use the auxiliary *être* in compound tenses.

General instructions regarding the conjugations of reflexive verbs can be found on pages 21 and 22. Specific conjugation patterns for regular *-er*, *-ir*, or *-re* verbs or irregular verbs can be found on the pages indicated after each of the following verbs.

s'amuser to have fun, 7	**se marier** to get married, 7
s'appeler to be called, 32	**se passer** to happen, 7
s'arrêter to stop, 7	**se passer de** to do without, 7
s'asseoir to sit down, 35	**se porter** to feel (health), 7
s'en aller to go away, 35	**se promener** to go for a walk, 32
s'endormir to fall asleep, 37	**se rappeler** to remember, 32
s'ennuyer to get bored, 32	**se reposer** to rest, 7
s'habiller to get dressed, 7	**se retourner** to turn around, 7
se blesser to hurt oneself, 7	**se réveiller** to wake up, 7
se brosser to brush (one's hair), 7	**se sentir** to feel (health or emotion), 40
se coucher to go to bed, 7	**se servir de** to use, 40
se demander to wonder, 7	**se souvenir** to remember; 41, 42
se dépêcher to hurry, 7	**se taire** to be quiet, 41
se déshabiller to get undressed, 7	**se tromper** to be mistaken, 7
se fâcher to get mad, 7	**se trouver** to be (located or found), 7
se faire mal to get hurt, 38	**se vanter** to boast, 7
se laver to wash (oneself), 7	
se lever to get up, 32	

Reflexive or pronominal verbs may also be used for reciprocal actions to show action passing from one person to another: *se rencontrer* (to meet each other). The following verbs are commonly used in that fashion:

s'écrire to write to each other, 37	**se donner** to give to each other, 7
s'entendre to get along with each other, 9	**se parler** to speak to each other, 7
	se rencontrer to meet each other, 7
s'offrir to offer to each other, 39	**se réunir** to meet with each other, 8
se battre to fight with each other, 35	**se téléphoner** to call each other, 7
se comprendre to understand each other, 40	**se voir** to see each other, 42